HAIKU

INSPIRATIONS

HAIKU

INSPIRATIONS

TOM LOWENSTEIN WITH VICTORIA JAMES

POEMS AND MEDITATIONS
ON NATURE AND BEAUTY

CHARTWELL
BOOKS, INC.

Haiku Inspirations
Tom Lowenstein
with Victoria James

Managing Editor: Kirsten Chapman
Editor: Zoë Fargher
Managing Designer: Daniel Sturges
Designer: Rebecca Johns
Picture Researcher: Susannah Stone
Commissioned artworks: Jeremy Sancha
Commissioned calligraphy: Yukki Yaura

1 3 5 7 9 10 8 6 4 2

This edition published in 2013 by
CHARTWELL BOOKS, INC.
A division of BOOK SALES, INC.
276 Fifth Avenue Suite 206
New York, New York 10001
USA

First published in the
United Kingdom and Ireland in 2006 by
Duncan Baird Publishers, an imprint of
Watkins Publishing Limited
Sixth Floor, 75 Wells Street,
London W1T 3QH

A member of Osprey Group

A CIP record for this book is available from the British Library

Typeset in Bembo
Color reproduction by Scanhouse, Malaysia
Printed in China by Imago

ISBN: 978-0-7858-2979-9

Contents

Introduction

Of all the styles of Japanese poetry published in English translation, haiku is undoubtedly the best known and most loved. I was first inspired by the haunting beauty and inexhaustible variety of haiku when I taught poetry many years ago in an inner-city school. It was the sheer brevity of the haiku form that initially drew me to try teaching what was then an exotic genre, but the experiment with these short poems in English translation was bewilderingly successful. To my gratification, poems by long-dead Buddhists from a remote island, about full moons, melancholy autumn nights and plum blossom reached the children's imagination as vividly as did poems by the same writers about birds, frogs and blood-gorged mosquitoes disturbing their meditation.

This experience illustrates an intriguing fact about haiku: that the exquisite sensibility that responds to the indefinable melancholy of moonlight can also be humorous, ribald and, not least, in lively touch with the little creatures and daily events that variously amuse or harass human beings the world over. Haiku poets embraced these paradoxical extremes, and expressed them with the uncluttered sensitivity of children, giving haiku its subtle but sprightly magic.

Bell chimes fade,
and the scent of blossom
spreads in the twilight.

———————————

BASHŌ

Out of the way, little sparrow!
Make yourself scarce!
Mr Horse is coming through!

———————————

ISSA

Structure and form

The art of haiku is not, of course, child's play – writers in
the Japanese tradition spend years perfecting their technique.
In their strictest form, haiku consist of only "essential" words,
and contain 17 syllables (though Japanese and English ideas
of a syllable are not equivalent). A classic haiku is three lines
long, made up of 5–7–5 "syllables". It also contains a *kigo*
(season word; see pages 116–19), which suggests the mood
and atmosphere governing the poem. The *kigo* can be simply
the word for the season, or allude indirectly to a season that
the reader can easily identify – rain, blossom and young grass
suggest the joyful days of spring, while the moon and lonely
pine trees suggest the melancholy of autumn, and so on.

Finally, a traditional haiku should include a *kireji* (cutting
word) such as *ya*, *kana* or *keri*. Placed at the end of any of the
lines, *kireji* have no translatable meaning, but denote a pause
or a full stop – their presence implies a moment to reflect on
the preceding line(s). Some haiku writers, such as the early
19th-century poet Issa, took pleasure in violating these rules,
and indeed the late 19th-century poet Shiki specifically
advised beginners to forget the old rules of grammar.

Origins and development

Haiku almost certainly evolved from *tanka* (short poems), also called *waka* (Japanese poems). These are 31-syllable poems structured in five lines (5–7–5–7–7 syllables), developed by court poets during the Heian period (794-1185). Individual courtiers during this golden age of the arts used Japanese poetry to display their imaginative wit, to advance their careers in the imperial city, and as a means of communication. They also experimented with improvised group compositions that extended *tanka* into *renga* (linked verses). *Renga* were written by groups taking their cue from a *hokku* (an opening verse, or "seed"), which was 17 syllables long, had a 5–7–5 syllable structure, and was usually the work of the writing circle's host or most accomplished poet. The *hokku* was regarded as the most significant part of the *renga*: it established a seasonal setting, and suggested a mood and an emotion around which the other writers invented and embroidered. By the 15th century *hokku* sometimes formed independent poems, which resembled what we know today as haiku.

During the 16th century increasing literacy led to the invention of a lighter, more humorous and colloquial style of *renga*, known as *haikai no renga*. Hugely popular, these became increasingly over clever or naturalistic to the point of vulgarity. It was not until the late 17th century that poets such as Matsuo Bashō (1644–94) forged a poetic idiom in which stylistic elegance could be combined with colloquial language to create haiku that were both as exquisite as *tanka* and accessible to non-literary people. Poets including Taniguchi Buson (1715–83) (pages 62–3) and Kobayashi Issa (1762–1826) (pages 66–7) continued this tradition, but after their deaths haiku poetry again lost its way until Masaoka Shiki (1867–1902) (pages 69–70) revived and redefined the genre in the late 19th century. It was Shiki who originally distinguished the terms *hokku* and haiku, defining *hokku* as a literary term for the first verse of *renga*, and describing independent three-line poems as haiku. Today the terms haiku and *hokku* are largely interchangeable, so for ease of reference we describe all the poems in this book as haiku.

Aesthetic reverence

A veritable "cult of beauty" (see page 46) informed much Japanese poetry from the Heian period through to the haiku

Spring rain.
And these little frogs'
bellies still aren't wet.

BUSON

Moorland grasses
swaying, swaying,
as spring passes.

ISSA

writers of the 17th and 18th centuries and beyond. Profound love of the varied and dramatic Japanese landscape, allied to sensitivity to the vividly changing seasons, had been important to Japanese people at least since the sixth to eighth centuries AD, from which period the earliest anthology of Japanese poems, the *Man'yōshū* (*The Collection of Many Leaves*), survives. In the *Man'yōshū*, which contains more than 4,000 poems, many delightful short pieces evoke nature or situate the writer within a beautiful landscape. In one poem (the top example on this page), a seventh-century prince exclaims happily at the approach of spring while skilfully focusing on rock, water and fern buds. A joyful folk song (bottom example) from the same early period suggests that ordinary people shared this love of the natural world.

Similar folk songs formed part of Shinto religious rituals, and the ancient Japanese religion of nature played a vivid role in the country's aesthetic life. As described later (pages 76–9), Shinto has from early times celebrated the power and the beauty of nature, and in Shinto-inspired Heian poetry we first find the observational sharpness and concision that informed haiku written hundreds of years later.

Above the torrent
rushing down the rocks
the bracken is budding,
and spring is upon us!

AUTHOR UNKNOWN

Snow falls and deepens
on bamboo grass,
but how lovely to dance!

AUTHOR UNKNOWN

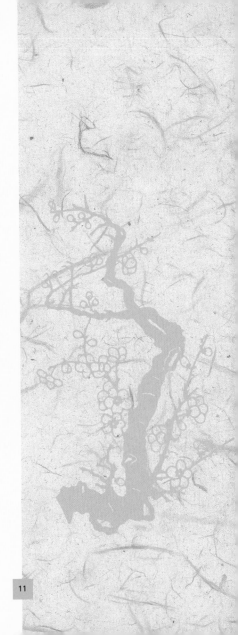

Buddhism and transience

Buddhism, which entered Japan in the sixth century, and particularly the doctrine that life is characterized by the impermanence of all worldly things, also played a key role in the development of haiku. While Buddhism in India had suggested that beauty, on account of its impermanence, was of little importance, Japanese Buddhists, in particular those who practised Zen, developed an appreciation for the way in which beauty and transience coexisted, and deployed images such as dewdrops and cherry blossom to imply that things might be beautiful partly *because* they were impermanent. The term *aware* (sadness) was used often in art and poetry from the Heian period onward, and the courtly tradition of *mono no aware* (the pathos of things) described the way in which life was tinged with a constant sorrow that was also aesthetically delicious.

Many of the greatest haiku poets – including Bashō, Buson and Issa, each of whom is represented in this book – were devout Buddhists, and many of their poems contain appropriately poignant visions of dewdrop-like transience in the *ukiyo* (floating world) – a frequently used term for our fragile, dreamlike social and natural environment. Buson expressed this with elegant and painterly precision (see the top haiku on this page), while Bashō, who loved travelling through rural Japan, often evoked mortality by subtle reference to ancient history (as in the bottom haiku).

The essence of haiku

Finally, it is worth quoting two statements that can enhance our appreciation of the haiku in this book. The first defines the term *yugen*, a word that describes a suggestion of the unseen, of what lies beneath the surface. "*Yugen*," wrote Kamo no Chōmei in the early 13th century, "is an overtone that does not appear in words … . The evening sky in autumn has no colour, no voice. But still you find tears welling up in your eyes … . It is what lies behind that enchants you …" Haiku poetry should be full of *yugen*, touching the heart, and leading the reader to a profound and moving appreciation of nature, emotion – even life itself.

The second statement comes from Bashō's words as recorded by his students about contact with and observation of nature. "To learn about the pine tree," said the master, "you

Camellia petals drop

spilling

yesterday's rain.

BUSON

Summer grass:

that's all that remains

of warriors' dreams.

BASHŌ

must go to the pine tree." A pine tree simply "is", and a poet should experience the things of the world not in the light of his own thoughts about them, but on their own terms. "Otherwise," said Bashō in the same discourse, "you impose yourself on the object and do not learn. Poetry emerges when you and the object become as one. When you enter that object deeply, its hidden essence (*kyo*) will reveal itself."

This book is intended to offer an introduction to haiku poetry, complemented with background on the history and culture of Japan. Although the natural world and everyday events are the predominant subjects of the haiku we have chosen, haiku poets also touch on religious, social, historical and cultural themes and, more importantly, these contexts would have informed and influenced the poets. The haiku are offered not to illustrate the accompanying texts and images, but as poems to appreciate in their own right. We hope that these short poems will reveal their "hidden essence" to the reader, and offer something of the inspiration that generated their original composition.

Tom Lowenstein

Society and Court Life

Japan's Heian period (794–1185) saw an intense artistic flowering, centred on the imperial court at Heian-kyō (modern-day Kyoto). Elegant manners and elaborate costume were admired by the court, which also produced beautiful and enduring literature and visual art. Among the courtiers love poetry flourished, and both women and men became acclaimed and popular authors of poetry and prose.

Two courtiers traverse a narrow mountain pass in this 18th-century screen painting by Fukae Roshu.

The Heian period

The golden age of Japanese arts started in 794 AD, when the imperial court settled in a new capital city. Heian-kyō, "the City of Peace", later called Kyoto, was beautifully sited and symmetrically laid out, and for the next thousand years would be the Japanese capital.

The Heian period was one of cultural and social isolation. For the two previous centuries, the Japanese people had borrowed enthusiastically from China, and ideas about statecraft, religion and the visual and literary arts were all largely based on Chinese models. But in 894 the imperial court ceased to have official relations with China, and the century that followed saw the consolidation of a Kyoto-based culture whose identity became increasingly national – for example, enthusiasm for *kanshi* (Chinese poetry) waned in favour of *waka* (poetry in Japanese).

The glory of Heian society lay in its devotion to the arts. Literature, calligraphy and the visual arts – all promoted and often practised by the emperor himself – flourished. However, the arts remained the exclusive preoccupation of a leisured aristocracy, or "the good people", as opposed to the masses who were characterized as "mere people". The "good people"

Power behind the throne

At the centre of Heian life was the person of the emperor. A strict courtly etiquette surrounded him, and this radiated from the court into society at large, helping to create wider stability. However, the actual political power was in the hands of one aristocratic family, the Fujiwaras (see pages 24–5), who successfully retained control of government for more than two centuries by marrying their daughters into the imperial family.

expended vast amounts of time on ceremonies and festivals. Both Shinto and Buddhist festivals were celebrated, and it was a mark of Heian serenity that these two very different systems could develop alongside one another so peacefully.

Courtly refinement was also evident in the conduct of love affairs, as liaisons outside marriage were accepted in the Heian court. Women and men lived separately, and a passionate courtship might be triggered by the glimpse of a trailing kimono sleeve, or of a lady's sleek black hair.

Above: A detail of a c.13th-century illustration from the *Diary of Lady Murasaki*, showing a moonlit boat ride. Such romantic excursions were common among Heian courtiers, who might take the opportunity to compose poetry, or fall in love.

Kyoto, Tokyo and Osaka

Five great cities have shaped Japan's history – Kamakura, Kyoto, Nara, Osaka and Tokyo. Today Nara and Kamakura are still blessed with a wealth of cultural treasures, but have become quiet provincial towns. Tokyo and Osaka remain great commercial and administrative centres. Although now built largely of concrete, both cities have historic districts of great charm, including traditional *shitamachi* (low town) areas where the centuries slip away down winding streets lined with low wooden houses. But only Kyoto has retained both beauty and administrative importance.

Kyoto literally means "capital city", and the city is still the cultural centre of Japan. The imperial court originally moved from Nara to Kyoto – then called Heian-kyō – in 794 in order to escape the controlling influence of the Nara Buddhist clergy and their powerful monasteries. Kyoto remained the seat of the imperial court from 794 until 1868.

However, at the end of the Heian period (1185), political power shifted to Kamakura, seat of the Minamoto shoguns, who considered Kyoto court life to be irredeemably decadent and corrupt. After the ruling shogun was overthrown and Kamakura was burnt down in 1333, the government moved

Opposite: A bustling street and the exterior of a draper's store in Edo (modern-day Tokyo).

back to Kyoto, and the city and its cultural heritage survived intact several political upheavals that followed.

Kyoto was spared bombing raids during World War II, and today the city is famed for its extraordinary wealth of temples and gardens. There are 1,600 Buddhist temples, 400 Shinto shrines and 17 UNESCO world heritage sites. Cultural traditions such as *geisha*, *ikebana* (Japanese flower arranging) and tea ceremony continue to thrive there.

The stories of Tokyo and Osaka are hardly less remarkable. Named Edo, meaning "estuary", the eastern settlement that became Tokyo was just a village until the region's overlord constructed a castle there in the mid-15th century. In 1590 the castle passed into the hands of Tokugawa Ieyasu, and Edo became his administrative centre when he assumed power as shogun in 1603, the beginning of the Edo period.

Although never a place of artistic innovation equal to Kyoto, Edo was a powerful cultural and political centre, not least thanks to the *sankin kotai* system of "alternate residence", whereby powerful *daimyō* (warlords) were compelled to spend alternating years in Edo and in their home domain, while their wives and children had to reside constantly in Edo. This system ensured the loyalty of the *daimyō* to the ruling shogun, and meant that each *daimyō* maintained several residences, which created a class of wealthy, discriminating patrons in Tokugawa-era Edo. By the 18th century the population of Tokyo was more than 1 million – the world's largest at the time. Today home to some 28 million, the Tokyo-Yokohama area remains the world's most populous metropolis.

Osaka's fortune was also decided by a castle. The city was a backwater port until, in the 16th century, Toyotomi Hideyoshi (see page 32) built a mighty fortress there. In the subsequent years of peace under Tokugawa rule, and aided by its position on the delta formed by the Yamato and Yodo rivers, Osaka expanded as an international mercantile centre, bankrolling the cultural excess of its near-neighbour, Kyoto.

From the 17th century onward, Osaka was a centre of trade. The Genroku period, a flowering of popular culture between 1688 and 1704, focused on the Kyoto-Osaka region. It was the merchants of Osaka who most enthusiastically embraced *bunraku* (puppet theatre) and the *sewamono* genre of realistic drama (see pages 148–9). Today Osaka is second only to Tokyo in industrial and commercial importance.

Twilight

in the middle of the town.

A single butterfly.

Takarai Kikaku

—————————————

The moon is cold.

The bridge echoes

as I cross alone.

Tan Taigi

梨

梨
の
花
月
に
文
読
む
女
あ
り

The pear tree is in blossom.

In the moonlight

a woman reads a letter.

BUSON

Emperors

Emperor Akihito, the present incumbent of the Chrysanthemum Throne, is Japan's 125th emperor in a line said to have been unbroken for more than 1,500 years.

According to legend, the first emperor of Japan was Jimmu, enthroned in 660BC, a descendant of the sun goddess Amaterasu, daughter of Izanagi and his sister-consort Izanami, the divinities who created the world. This story is the origin of the claim to divinity of the Japanese imperial line.

The first major imperial epoch was the reign of Prince Shōtoku (574-622), who exercised power while his mother, Empress Suiko, held the throne. Shōtoku reshaped Japanese culture, religion and government after Chinese models.

Emperors ruled Japan (at least ceremonially) first from Nara, then from Heian-kyō (now Kyoto). Before the mid-ninth century, the emperors themselves had full political control. In 858, however, nine-year-old Seiwa ascended the throne. His maternal grandfather, Fujiwara Yoshifusa, took power and revived the post of *sesshu* (chancellor), which he retained even after Seiwa reached adulthood. Yoshifusa passed the post to his son, who in turn created the new post of *kampaku* (regent). The Fujiwara family dominated political life during the Heian period through their hold on these two offices, gaining a stranglehold on power that peaked with Fujiwara Michinaga (966-1028), who married four out of his five daughters to emperors, and was grandfather to three.

In 1068 Emperor Go-Sanjo, who was not born of a Fujiwara mother, ascended the throne and the Fujiwara grip on power failed. Go-Sanjo devised the *insei* (cloistered government) system of rule, whereby an abdicated monarch governed by controlling a puppet ruler, often his son, who occupied the throne. This system lasted until 1192, when social upheaval brought to power a new ruler, shogun Minamoto no Yoritomo, and a new capital, Kamakura. For the next 700 years, military men ruled Japan, though an emperor remained always on the throne.

This period came to an end in 1868, when a group of ambitious oligarchs overthrew the tottering Tokugawa shogunate and restored the emperor to the position of head of state – the so-called Meiji restoration. Although Emperor Hirohito renounced his claim to immortality in January 1946, and Japan is now a constitutional democracy, the imperial family remains the symbolic heart of the nation.

Opposite: The chrysanthemum (top) and the paulownia (bottom) have been crests of the Japanese imperial throne for at least 1,000 years. Chrysanthemum petals resemble the rays of the sun, while according to myth the sacred *houou* (phoenix) would alight and nest only in the paulownia, or Empress tree. Both are thus seen as symbols of longevity, or even immortality.

Life at Court

Ritual and ceremony filled the day-to-day life of the Heian courtier, while the arts of political and romantic intrigue were as essential as those of poetry and music. Religious observances, seasonal festivals and state occasions such as birth, marriage and funerals gave structure to the court year. Both men and women also made pilgrimages from the capital to nearby holy places.

Court life was largely sedentary. Days were filled with pursuit of the arts and genteel pastimes. Board games such as *go* (see pages 28–9), *shogi* (chess) and *sugoroku* (backgammon) were popular, as was *kaiawase*, an elegant version of snap, in which players matched pairs of painted seashells. Another game involved identifying and matching incense by scent.

Rarer, more active court pursuits included *yabusame* (horseback archery). Also played was *kemari*, a form of soccer in which there are no teams and no winner, the objective being merely to pass the ball – suggestive, perhaps, of the consensus-driven ethos that still pervades Japanese life.

Certain qualities were revered at the Heian court: *makoto* (sincerity), *aware* (sadness) and *miyabi* (courtliness). *Mono no aware* (the pathos of things) was the defining sensibility.

Opposite: This 13th-century scroll shows Sugawara Michizane (845–903) as a youth practising archery with other nobles. Michizane was a poet, scholar and statesman who was exiled from Kyoto to the island of Kyushu, mainly because he presented a threat to the powerful Fujiwara clan. He died in exile, and a strange series of calamities – storms, fires and violent death – beset the capital, thought to have been caused by Michizane in revenge. To appease the angry spirit, he was deified as a Shinto *kami*, Tenjin, and a shrine to him stands at Kitano in Kyoto.

Go

Perhaps the world's oldest continually played board game, *go*'s recorded origins date back to China in the sixth century BC. Today *go* is also the most played board game worldwide, with an estimated 100 million enthusiasts.

Go's modern popularity is ironic, as it was traditionally the game of the élite – common folk played chess. In ancient China mastery of *go* was one of the "four refinements" of a scholar, the other three being calligraphy, ink painting and accomplishment on the *guqin* (a silk-string zither).

Although the game originated in China, where it is named *wei-qi*, it is known today by its Japanese title. It entered Japan around 740. Initially the preserve of court circles, the game quickly found favour with both Buddhist and Shinto clergy.

With simple rules, but requiring complex strategy, *go* is played with black or white counters called stones on a square grid composed of 19 × 19 lines. The black player goes first, and players take it in turn to place their stones at unoccupied line intersections, of which there are 361 on the board. When one or more stones are surrounded by stones of the opposing colour , they are "captured" and removed from the board, though they may be replaced later. The game ends when both players pass on their turn, and the score is calculated. Each captured stone or surrounded line intersection counts as one point, though the player who moved first has five points deducted, to make up for his "opening-move advantage".

Widely played in Japan by the 13th century, *go* was adopted by samurai. By 1612 the governing military regime had recognized the usefulness of *go* as a game of strategy, and the first *go* academy was opened under the aegis of Honinbo Sansa, the country's best player. Around the same time other top-ranked *go* families were awarded grants to promote the game and train players, and such competition improved player performance. In the 1670s the Honinbo School was headed by its fourth master, Dosaku, perhaps the greatest player in *go*'s history, who greatly advanced the game's theory.

In 1868, reflecting Japan's drive to Westernize, official support for the *go* academies was withdrawn. Since then the game has endured uneven fortunes. However, the formation of the Japan *Go* Association in the 1920s, along with *go* competitions sponsored by newspapers, *go manga* (comics) and the recent invention of online playing, have ensured the game's continued popularity.

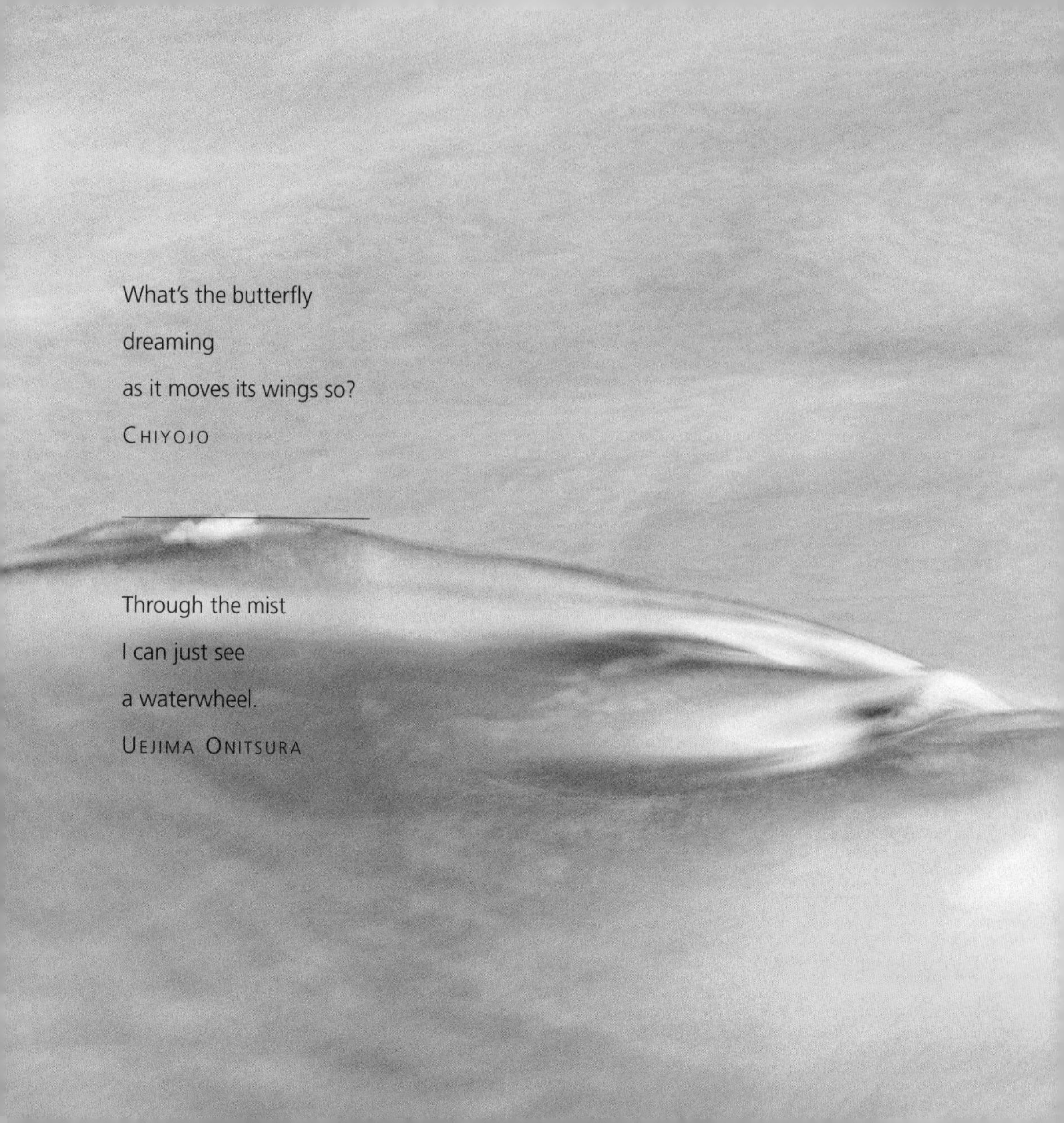

What's the butterfly

dreaming

as it moves its wings so?

CHIYOJO

Through the mist

I can just see

a waterwheel.

UEJIMA ONITSURA

朝霧

朝霧や
孫/\まのく
夢の
人どきくり

Hazy morning:
as in a painting of a dream,
the people passing.

BUSON

Warfare

The Heian period, a golden age of peace and stability that enabled art and culture to flourish, eventually collapsed into civil war between the mighty Taira and Minamoto dynasties. The Taira seized power first, only to lose it to the Minamoto at the sea battle of Dan-no-Ura in 1185.

Aside from the failed invasion by Kublai Khan, all Japan's great wars during the medieval period were fought within its own borders, and internal strife during the 13th and 14th centuries was protracted and bloody. Khan's fleet sailed twice but was each time rebuffed by a storm, the *kamikaze* (divine wind) – a name adopted by the suicide pilots of World War II.

The Ashikaga shoguns, great patrons of the arts, ruled from 1336 until 1467, but in that year the country was plunged into the decade-long Ōnin War. There followed a century of civil war known simply as the *Sengoku Jidai* (the Warring States period), when various factions vied for control.

Real peace did not return to Japan until around 1568, when the powerful warlord Oda Nobunaga (1534–82) began the long process of Japanese unification. He and two other great warlords, Toyotomi Hideyoshi (1536-98) and Tokugawa Ieyasu (1543-1616), brought order out of chaos.

Literature and Drama

The struggle between the Taira and Minamoto clans inspired the *Heike Monogatari* (*Tale of the Heike*), which rivals *The Tale of Genji* (see page 38) for pre-eminence in the Japanese literary pantheon. Additionally, the rivalry between the first Minamoto shogun, Yoritomo, and his half-brother Yoshitsune is a staple of both *kabuki* and *noh* dramas.

Right: A battle unfolds, in a detail from a handscroll painted during the military Kamakura period (1185–1333).

Samurai

Synonymous with Japanese militarism and chivalry, the hereditary samurai warrior class came into being in the 12th century. A boy would receive his first sword at the age of five, and spend his childhood building manly courage – playing barefoot in the snow, for example. By their early teens young samurai were expected to have mastered etiquette, and at 13 they would begin their military training, which lasted nine years. Rejection of a samurai birthright was rare, but one man who did so was Matsuo Bashō (see pages 56–9), the great haiku writer, who chose the life of a wandering poet-monk.

Samurai adhered to the code of *bushidō* (the way of the warrior). The notion is nearly impossible to codify – it was never written down – but at its heart lie such notions as justice, loyalty, fearlessness, benevolence and frugality.

During the long years of Tokugawa peace (1603–1868), samurai became little more than bureaucrats, but they went out in a blaze of glory – the Satsuma Rebellion of 1876-7. In this revolt led by Saigo Takamori, 20,000 warriors clashed with 60,000 government troops trained in modern warfare. Defeated, Saigo and his 300 samurai committed *seppuku* (ritual suicide). Today they are revered as national heroes.

The 47 rōnin

Rōnin are masterless samurai. *Chushingura* (*Tale of The 47 Rōnin*) tells of a warlord, Asano, who wounded fellow *daimyō* Kira in the presence of the shogun. Asano was ordered to commit *seppuku* for his disrespect. Nearly two years later, 47 of his samurai stormed Kira's stronghold and beheaded him in revenge. They confessed to the shogun, who had no alternative but to order them to commit *seppuku*, which they did with unquestioning obedience. The rōnin and Asano were interred at Sengaku-ji temple in Tokyo, and are honoured there today.

Left: A fierce samurai wields his sword in a blizzard in this 19th-century woodblock print. A samurai's sword was his most precious possession, and the weapon itself was symbolic of the warrior class – only samurai were allowed to wear them.

Boat

left at the inlet

frozen outside and inside.

Nozawa Bonchō

———————————————

Beneath a hazy moon:

downstream, the sound

of a net cast on the river.

Tan Taigi

梅

うめ咲くや帯買ふ室の遊女ぶ

Plum blossom time.
Courtesans buying sashes
in their houses of pleasure.
BUSON

Women of culture

A Japanese woman of the Heian court, Lady Murasaki Shikibu, wrote one of the world's first novels – the *Tale of Genji* (*c*.1002). In the Heian period women's lives, reflecting the cultural sophistication of the era, became extraordinarily refined in artistic pursuits, costume and behaviour.

The most privileged women were often the unhappiest. Heian court women produced the first masterpieces of Japanese vernacular literature, and they also left a number of *nikki* (diaries). Despite espousing the high-flown ideals of *miyabi* (courtliness), the Heian world portrayed in diaries such as the *Kagero Nikki* (*The Gossamer Years*) did not value women highly, and many noblewomen suffered abandonment and loneliness in their cloistered quarters.

Perhaps the most familiar embodiment of historical Japanese feminine grace and accomplishment is the *geisha* (person of arts), who appeared in the mid-18th century. Unlike the Heian court, the world of a *geisha* was based on sisterhood. The teahouses where *geisha* worked were overseen by an *okāsan* (mother), more experienced *geisha* were termed *onēsan* (older sister) and a ritual, the *sansan kudo,* bound a *geisha* and her apprentice *maiko* in bonds of sisterhood.

Below: Skilled courtesans entertain with dance and musical instruments including the three-stringed *shamisen*, in this 19th-century woodblock print.

Distinct from courtesans, who provided sexual services, the *geisha* were prized for their knowledge of the arts. *Geisha* were style-setting celebrities, but were also regarded as spiritually refined, owing to the close connection between the practice of the Japanese arts and the pursuit of spiritual perfection.

Kimonos

The kimono was worn daily in Japan for almost 2,000 years, and remained the everyday wear of choice until the end of the 19th century, during the rapid Westernization following the Meiji restoration in 1868.

In the early Heian period, the court adopted an elaborate colour-coding by rank that distinguished the outfits of courtiers and government officials – a practice found in ancient China. The permitted colours were purple, blue, red, yellow, white and black. The use of certain colours was restricted by complex symbolism – for example, the bright pink *kurenai,* the colour of the transient cherry blossom, was used only by the highest-ranking court ladies.

Garments were multilayered and sleeves fell well over the hands – not least because of the extreme chill of the Japanese winter, endured in wood-and-paper buildings. Women wore up to 20 layers at a time, though the official name for such garments was *junihito* (12-layered). These luxurious clothes were so heavy that women often "walked" on their knees because it was too difficult to stand. The trailing sleeve became a motif in love poetry, in which women wept into their sleeves over a faithless or absent lover.

In later centuries, as politics turned turbulent, dress was more austere and practical. But during the Edo period, with the Tokugawa restoration of peace and growing affluence in urban centres, Japanese dress once more broke out in a riot of colour and luxury. Advanced techniques such as the *yuzen* (dye-resist) process meant that complex patterns could be created on silk. For the first time the *obi*, which sashed the waist, was tied at the back not the front, and elaborate bows and knots were favoured. Men adopted *hakama*, skirt-like trousers with seven pleats, each representing one of the seven virtues of *bushidō*, the way of the warrior.

This Edo style of kimono is the one still worn today, by both women and men. While few Japanese favour kimonos for everyday wear, traditional dress is still worn for occasions such as Coming-of-Age Day and pursuits such as tea ceremony. In recent years a simplified version of the *yukata* (cotton summer kimono) has enjoyed renewed popularity.

Snow melts

and the village overflows

with children.

ISSA

_____

Every patch of water

in the rice fields

frozen this morning.

NOZAWA BONCHŌ

吹雪

ゆくりなく騎
面もふらず
吹雪の中

Eleven men on horses

ride steadily forward

through the wind and snow storm.

SHIKI

The Poet's World

Some of the earliest Japanese poetry has the brevity and visual beauty later associated with haiku. Folk songs, and poems written at the Heian court, express delight in nature and depths of feeling that were also evident in the haiku written by poets of the 17th and 18th centuries. Many of the greatest haiku poets were Buddhists, who expressed their vision of the world through their poetry.

A detail from a manuscript album of haiku poems accompanied by drawings. The appearance of the solitary, elusive heron was considered a good omen.

The cult of beauty

An appreciation of the arts and the cultivation of exquisite courtly manners were equally important to the lives of Kyoto aristocrats during Japan's Heian period. While aesthetic refinement in life and the arts was largely the preserve of the élite, and many aspects of taste had originally been borrowed from China, a love of sheer beauty had been given a distinctively Japanese complexion as early as the eighth century with the *Man'yōshū* (see page 10) a collection of poems characterized by deep feeling, sensibility and colourful imagery. The *Man'yōshū* was compiled by courtiers and featured pieces by famous aristocrats, but among its 4,000 poems are pieces by anonymous peasants and soldiers.

By the tenth century it was assumed that high-born Kyoto people would be connoisseurs and practitioners of arts including music, calligraphy and poetry. Poetry was a daily pursuit, and courtiers were under pressure from the court to produce poems to mark significant events. The poem itself was only one component of its aesthetic worth. Calligraphy, choice of paper, the artfulness of its folding, the flower accompanying it – even the appearance of the messenger who delivered it – all conspired to define the value of its beauty.

Right: A lady admires her reflection at a *ryokan* (inn) at an *onsen* (hot spring). She is dressed in a traditional *yukata* (summer kimono). The waters at *onsen* are said to promote beauty and health, and they remain extremely popular.

Society and solitude

From as early as the tenth century, many Japanese poets became preoccupied by two contrasting experiences: the demands of social life versus the pleasures of solitude.

Courtiers during the Heian period used poetry instead of ordinary prose letters as a means of social communication. It was also composed in *renga* (linked verses) by groups of writers surrounding a master poet. However, poetry, like meditation, could be a medium of spiritual experience, and haiku poets' writing often emerged from a solitary, meditative poetic mood that they actively cultivated. For many writers, poetry was a sacred discipline.

Buddhist ideas that reached Japan from China were largely responsible for this ideal. The life and work of Chinese Zen poet Han Shan (*c.* eighth to ninth centuries), who abandoned society to "sing madly in the mountains", had significant influence. His "madness" was really spiritual joy, and the Japanese poet Bashō similarly described his own departure on a journey as "ecstasy in the moonlight". But detachment from society could also lead to loneliness – after his departure, Bashō described himself as a "weather-beaten skeleton … painfully afflicted by the autumn wind."

A melancholy mood

Sabi is a word that alludes to the solitary contemplative condition in which poetry is written, or to a lonely mood, feeling, colour or atmosphere. Bashō (see pages 56–9) sought out places that expressed the quality of *sabi*, such as the tumbledown House of the Fallen Persimmons near Kyoto where he spent some time in 1691, contemplating nature and the passage of time.

Opposite: This view of an isolated tree on a riverbank was painted in 15th-century China.

Green herbs

grow green

in the snowy meadow.

KONISHI RAIZAN

————————————

Watching the stars

through willow branches

makes me feel lonely.

MIURA CHORA

月に出に
草も風吹く
時鳥

時鳥

Moon behind the grasses.

Wind blows through.

The cry of a cuckoo.

SHIKI

Poetic interludes

Many Japanese books from as early as the tenth century combined prose narrative and poetry. In many of these the poems served to create meditative breaks within a story, or to deepen perceptions that the prose had introduced.

Although there were precise rules governing most poetic composition (see pages 8–10), which could lead to artificiality, writing poems came naturally to educated people of the tenth century. Embedded within *The Tale of Genji*, Lady Murasaki Shikibu's fictional biography of a Heian-period courtier, are more than 800 poems, many ostensibly written by her characters. Most of these are "message poems" between friends and lovers that often reveal more subtle or profound emotions than a prose letter might be capable of expressing.

A lovely autobiographical book by a woman of the 11th century known as Lady Sarashina gives an account of a long and dangerous journey to Kyoto from a remote eastern province. Years later, when Lady Sarashina composed her story of this adventure, she inserted some of the poems that she and her companions had written along the way, and these both contribute to the narrative and help the reader to visualize what the travellers had stopped to contemplate.

Opposite: The Heian period author Sei Shonagon (seated). She is probably awaiting a lover – the poem which appears above her head tells of lovers meeting in the dead of night. In the poem "cocks' crows cause confusion", a subject echoed in the cockerel which appears on the screen to the right of the picture.

The *Pillow Book* of Sei Shonagon

S ei Shonagon (*c.*968–*c.*1025) was, from the age of
about 25, a maid of honour to one of the emperor's
consorts in the imperial city of Heian-kyō (Kyoto). She spent
most of her adult life at court and was a contemporary of
Lady Murasaki (see page 52). The two court ladies thoroughly
disliked one another, Murasaki declaring that Shonagon's
writing was "full of imperfections and frivolity".

The *Pillow Book* is actually a loosely constructed, non-
chronological diary, containing a mixture of observations,
court gossip, anecdote and curious lists of things Shonagon
liked and disliked. Gossipy as it sometimes is, the *Pillow Book*
is written in such exquisite prose that translator Arthur Waley
described Shonagon as "the best poet of her time".

No one knows the exact meaning of the term "pillow
book". While the codes for sexual behaviour at court were
relaxed, the title of Shonagon's book probably refers less to
an erotic purpose than to its function as bedside reading.
Shonagon's first entry offers a good example of the refined
quality of her sensibility. Describing what she likes about each
season, she notes how at dawn in spring "the light creeps over
the hills, their outlines being dyed a faint red while wisps of

purplish cloud trail over them". Although this description is recognizably Japanese, it is not necessarily what one would expect of a writer who spent most of her time in the seclusion of the court.

Much of what Shonagon admires belongs to the super-refined Heian culture of beautiful artefacts and correct behaviour, while what she hates is squalour and vulgarity. Her list of *Charming Things* thus describes how "Over a bright robe of beaten silk a lady's hair hangs neatly over her shoulders." By contrast, *Things That Are Unpleasant to See* include "Someone in a robe whose back seam is crooked."

Beauty and etiquette are also mutually identified in entries such as "Everyone should behave as elegantly as possible. Vulgar turns of speech are very bad." Likewise, she finds the way carpenters eat "most peculiar". In observations like these Shonagon gives eloquent expression to the rarefied élitism of the tenth-century aristocracy. Perhaps most endearing of her annotations are those that reflect her own idiosyncratic tastes: *Squalid Things* include "The inside of a cat's ear", whereas *Unsettling Things* include the wonderfully evocative "Eating strawberries in the dark."

The life of Bashō

J apan's greatest haiku poet was born near Kyoto in about 1644. His father was a minor samurai, and Bashō started his career as a page to another samurai in his home district. The samurai master was scarcely two years Bashō's senior, and the two young men together wrote fashionable verses and in 1664 published poems in a Kyoto anthology. Soon after Bashō began his service, his master died, and the young poet took to the road for a career of wandering and writing that continued until his death at the age of 50.

Bashō's brilliance as a poet soon earned him literary authority. In 1672 he edited an anthology by 30 other poets and, having moved to the city of Edo to find work or a patron among the nobility, he began to write and distribute new poems and judge poetry contests.

By now Bashō had his own students, and in 1681 some of these followers built him a modest hut on the outskirts of Edo. This solitary spot became the poet's home for the remainder of his life. A neighbour planted a *bashō* (banana tree) outside his hut in the spring of his arrival, and the poet, whose life was often as solitary and inconspicuous as this modest tree, became known as the "master of the Banana

Opposite: This 19th-century print shows Bashō pausing on one of his many journeys to share the mid-autumn Crescent Moon Festival with two farmers.

Plant Hut" – and from this came the poet's literary name, Bashō. In this hut, in monk-like simplicity, he received friends and admirers; from here he set out on his famous journeys through Japan. Not least, it was here that he sat, meditated and wrote many of his incomparable poems.

For much of Bashō's later life, he was torn between a melancholy solitude and engagement with friends and dependants. On the one hand he craved success through his writing, and on the other he sought enlightenment through meditation, in which he was instructed by a Zen priest who passed through Edo in the 1680s. In the stillness of his contemplation, Bashō's poetry expresses a profound grasp of "things as they are" in nature, uninterrupted by human interference. In his engagement with the world, Bashō also celebrates both the joys and sufferings of life's brief journey.

Bashō's travels

Bashō went on several important journeys on foot. When he embarked on his first journey in autumn 1684, Bashō was, as he later wrote in *The Record of a Weather-beaten Skeleton*, following the tradition of Japanese Buddhist pilgrims, who

Bashō's *haibun*

Bashō devised his own style of poetry and prose composition, known as *haibun*, which integrates verse and prose. Many of Bashō's *haibun* are travel journals with haiku embedded between prose paragraphs. Other *haibun* describe visits to nearby shrines or lonely cottages where Bashō considers his own humanity and questions the nature of the "wind-swept spirit" that inhabits his body, or compares himself to the plants and animals with which he shares the world.

started visiting shrines in their own country in the tenth century (see pages 98–9). While those pilgrims travelled with the purpose of winning religious salvation, Bashō took to the road both to explore, and to detach himself from the *ukiyo* (floating world) of existence and attain spiritual freedom.

Another aspect of Bashō's purpose was, however, literary and aesthetic. He took his second, shorter trip to view the harvest moon at a shrine near Edo, though the prose and poetry he composed about this quiet but dramatic event expressed religious joy as well as aesthetic pleasure.

Bashō's later and most celebrated diary, *The Narrow Road to the Deep North*, describes the poet's long and challenging journey of 1689 into the remote north of Japan's main island, Honshu. As in Bashō's earlier journals, the prose narrative encloses haiku, whose exquisite brevity distils his experience of landscapes, country people and events along the way. *The Narrow Road* opens with one of the poet's most exalted statements of this theme. All human beings, he wrote, "spend every moment of their lives travelling." And with that, Bashō strode forward into the "cloud-moving wind," becoming at one with all natural things that move toward extinction.

Cool, cool,

the wall against my heels

as I doze at midday.

BASHŌ

———————————

Irises blossom

over my feet –

blue sandal laces!

BASHŌ

浮世

露とくに洗みた浮世すゞばや

浮世すゞばや

How I would like
to wash the world's dust
with these dewdrops!
BASHŌ

Buson: poet and painter

B eautiful images are of the essence in haiku, and many of them evoke the varied natural beauty of Japan. Perhaps the most famous exponent of haiku after Bashō was the 18th-century poet Taniguchi Buson (1715–83), who combined the careers of haiku master and graphic artist.

Not only did Buson produce *haiga*, compositions that combine haiku and pictures, he also made a living as a painter, and his work, during his lifetime, became much in demand in both Edo and Kyoto. As his painting matured, Buson was able to practise both a conventional naturalism, and the long-neglected *nanga* style that Zen monks had brought from China in the 14th century. *Nanga* favoured free, intuitive brushstrokes, intended to capture the spirit of a subject rather than represent it literally.

Buson's haiku are similarly impressionistic in style, though he insisted to his students that "traditional rules of haiku must never be broken". Many of his poems evoke natural scenes, bringing exquisite colour and detail to the eye: the petals of a red flower pile up on each other as they fall; as a whale plunges mightily, its tail rises like a feather; morning dewdrops balance on the delicate hairs on a caterpillar's back.

Opposite: One of Buson's paintings, *Sight-seeing*, showing the poet contemplating a dramatic landscape. Many of Buson's poems display a profound appreciation for the mystery and wonder of nature, often expressed in visual images that show a painter's precision.

Spring rain falling.

On the roof a child's rag doll –

sodden.

BUSON

_____

It pierces my heel

as I walk in the bedroom:

my late wife's comb.

BUSON

桜ちる
苗代水や
星月夜

Cherry petals scattered
in the water between seedlings of rice:
moon and star light!

BUSON

Issa: the gentle rebel

"Issa opens his soul to us," wrote a commentator. "For this reason we love him." Issa (1762–1826) is lovable partly because he loved the world, and his writings radiate the compassion he felt for living beings. But his often joyful poems emerged from much desolate experience: his parents, two wives and all his children predeceased him.

Issa was ordained as a Buddhist priest of the Shin (Pure Land) sect and spent a decade as a homeless wanderer. While Bashō's experience of homelessness often evoked exalted metaphysical grandeur, Issa loved to write about the humble and ordinary – Issa, the priest's name he adopted, means "cup of tea," itself symbolic of his attachment to the everyday.

Known for his unkempt appearance and unconventional manners, Issa wrote poetry that was sometimes deliberately rough. He could deploy traditional images of cherry blossom and butterflies, but his playful imagination delighted in an all-embracing poetic vision of what was both exquisite and grubby: "Here comes a bush warbler! / Wiping his dirty feet / on the plum blossom." While this image suggests a rebellious break with refined literary aesthetics, a deep Buddhist insight informs Issa's vivid picture of transience and imperfection.

Red moon up there:

who does it belong to,

children?

ISSA

_____

Don't swat that fly:

it wrings its hands.

it wrings its feet.

ISSA

我とあそく

遊べや

親乃ない

すずめ

Come to me:

let's play

little sparrow orphan!

Issa

Shiki and the haiku revival

Masaoka Shiki was born in 1867, shortly before the Meiji restoration. His life thus coincided with a crucial period in Japanese history, when traditional Japanese values were challenged by and began to adapt to ideas from the West. Shiki died in 1902. Although he suffered constantly from ill-health, he wrote prolifically in his 35 short years, and is credited with successfully reviving the haiku genre.

Steeped in the haiku tradition since childhood, Shiki initially held political ambitions. Forced by illness to withdraw from the Imperial University in Tokyo, he joined the staff of the newspaper *Nihon* at the age of 25, where he became a high-profile journalist, and shocked the poetic establishment with a series of provocative articles. One of his most controversial essays was *Bashō Zatsudan* (*Criticism of Bashō*), in which he expressed the previously unthinkable idea that some of the master's poems were flawed. Shiki also advocated greater recognition for the poet Buson.

Shiki's main preoccupation was to free haiku from over-formality and artificiality. His newspaper columns contained revolutionary advice: "Forget grammar rules … write to please yourself …" These new ideas soon gathered a staunch following, formally recognized in 1895 as the Nihon School, which emphasized naturalistic, realistic writing. Shiki called his recommended technique *shasei* (sketch from life), and maintained that describing life just as it is, without too much reverence for old forms or artificially twisting the poem's structure and content, would produce the best haiku.

In 1897 Shiki established the literary magazine *Hototogisu* (*Cuckoo*), which took its name from his poem: "To ears / fatigued by preachers – / the cuckoo." Unlike Bashō, Buson and Issa, Shiki was agnostic, and this poem comments on the stagnancy of established orders, both in religion and poetry.

Under the strain of editing the magazine, along with personally reading the thousands of haiku submitted for publication, Shiki's health worsened, and he succumbed to the spinal tuberculosis that had threatened since his early 20s. Despite being bedridden, he continued to write poems and articles until two days before he died. Besides inspiring the haiku tradition with new spontaneity, Shiki's simple yet revolutionary aesthetic helped to redefine Japanese poetic expression for the modern era. It was Shiki, too, who coined the term haiku for the 17-syllable lyric poem we know today.

The thunder has subsided.

Evening sun on a single tree.

The cry of a cicada.

SHIKI

————————————————

Mounting through cloud

and breathing mist

the skylark soars.

SHIKI

稲妻

稲妻や
森のすき門に
稲妻

In a flash of summer lightning
through trees of the forest
I glimpsed water.
SHIKI

Symbol and Belief

The religions of Buddhism and
Shinto have coexisted in Japan
since the sixth century, each
informing and influencing the
other. While Shinto centres
on nature and celebrates
life cycles and the seasons,
Buddhism guides its followers
toward a life of meditation and
non-attachment. Temples,
pilgrimage, ritual and worship
have formed part of daily life
in Japan for hundreds of years.

The serene rock garden at the Nichiren
Buddhist Myorenji Temple in Kyoto.

Shinto

The ancient Japanese religion of nature, Shinto (the "way of the gods") probably evolved between the first and third centuries AD. In addition to its religious and ceremonial significance, Shinto has always expressed the Japanese people's appreciation of natural beauty.

Most Shinto "gods" are in fact *kami*, supernatural beings inhabiting trees, waterfalls or great rocks, whose shrines (see pages 110–13) are often sited in places of outstanding natural beauty. The clean, unadorned architecture of many of these shrines, which make use of plain wood and stone, has had a lasting influence on Japanese visual and literary arts.

In its earlier forms the Shinto religion was a loosely organized system. It had no priesthood, very little prescribed ritual, and Shinto writings, from the eighth century onward, consisted merely of descriptions of ceremonies and historical and mythological texts. Early Shinto ceremonies were intimately tied to natural cycles and to stages in human life.

After Buddhism arrived from China in the sixth century, Shinto and Buddhism adjusted to one another with great mutual tolerance. Many *kami* became identified with *buddhas* or *bodhisattvas*, saintly beings who renounce their own

Opposite: A Shinto shrine stands shrouded in mist on Mount Haguro, in the north of Honshu, Japan's main island. Along with Mount Gassan and Mount Yudono, Mount Haguro is one of the Dewa Sanzan (Three Sacred Mountains of Dewa), key sites for Shinto pilgrimage.

prospect of *nirvana* (by which souls are freed from the cycle of rebirth) in order to lead others toward enlightenment. The Shinto sun goddess Amaterasu herself came to be regarded as an esoteric aspect of the cosmic Buddha Vairocana.

Shinto practice varied according to region and social class. Peasant life was tied to Shinto festivals, which paid homage to the *kami* resident within their land to ensure good crops and to honour births, marriages and deaths. By the tenth century urban people lived within an cycle of increasingly numerous celebrations, particularly the Shinto *matsuri* (festivals) in Kyoto which surrounded the Emperor, who was believed to be a descendant of Amaterasu. Kyoto *matsuri* would often involve elaborate parades, with portable shrines carried through the city; while peasant rituals could be as simple as symbolically planting rice straw in the snowy fields on New Year's Day.

Shinto was the Japanese state religion from the Meiji restoration (1868) until Emperor Hirohito renounced his claim to immortality in 1946 and the constitution of 1947 prohibited the state's involvement in religion. Shinto returned to its earlier form – a loosely connected network of shrines dedicated to *kami*, many unique to the local communities.

Opposite: Meoto Iwa (the Wedded Rocks), at Futamigaura in Ise Bay. The rocks represent Izanagi and Izanami, the father and mother of the eight major islands of Japan, and of Shinto *kami* and deities including Amaterasu. The *shimenawa* (straw ropes) indicate that the rocks are sacred, and also symbolize the sanctity of the bond of marriage.

Mountain temple.

Image of Buddha entering nirvana.

No one comes to pay homage.

MIURA CHORA

_____

Under the rock

where I sit, legs folded,

a wisteria blossoms.

NAITO JŌSŌ

梅

静けさや
岩にしみ入る
せみの声

The silence of a temple.
The cry of a cicada
penetrates the rocks.
BASHŌ

Zen

The Japanese word *zen* comes from the Chinese *ch'an*; and this in turn derives from the ancient Indian Sanskrit term *dhyana*, meaning "meditation". Zen thus means the Buddhism of meditation: a radical path in which the rituals practised by other Buddhist schools are subordinated to silent personal effort.

Ch'an originated in sixth-century China and is said to have been introduced by the Indian monk Bodhidharma (*c.*450–*c.*530) who, according to legend, sat meditating in a cave for nine years before he was satisfied that he had achieved enlightenment. Bodhidharma's teaching derived from late Indian Mahayana Buddhist ideas, which contained the challenging doctrine that ultimate truth lay within the mind itself, and that everyone possessed this "Buddha nature". "Do not look for enlightenment or nirvana beyond your own mind," Bodhidharma taught his first followers.

Zen first arrived in Japan in the late 12th century. While Kyoto Buddhists remained faithful to earlier sects that had already developed a Japanese form, Zen was enthusiastically taken up in the north-east of the country by the Kamakura samurai caste.

Two schools

As in China, two main schools of Zen developed in Japan. Rinzai Zen emphasized meditation on *koans* – paradoxical stories and sayings (see page 91) designed to lead the mind beyond rational thought and thereby release it into an intuitive and direct knowledge without the interference of self or ego. A definitive form of Rinzai was systematized by the 18th-century master Hakuin, who was also an important poet, painter and calligrapher.

The other Japanese school of Zen was Soto, whose ideas were brought from China by the 12th-century monk Dōgen. Soto emphasised *zazen*, which means "just sitting" in meditation – a plain, straightforward and rigorous path that leads to a grasp of ultimate but unsayable knowledge. According to Buddhist ideals of non-attachment, suffering ends when we renounce our desire for worldly happiness and our dependence on notions of selfhood. Thus Dōgen also followed the earlier Buddhist technique of watching the breath – interpreting inhaling and exhaling as expressions of "not-self", because, as the Buddha himself taught, "There is no self to be attached to."

Previous page: The largest calligraphic character on this hanging scroll translates as "essence", a key concept in Zen. Calligraphy was often used as an aid to meditation.

Dōgen was a writer of genius whose works remain among the masterpieces of Japanese literature, and while he insisted that the truth of Zen lies beyond representation, thousands of practitioners have communicated Zen understanding in painting, poetry, calligraphy – even garden design.

Images of Zen

Ink-brush painting and calligraphy have long expressed the spiritual insight and energy of Far Eastern Buddhists. Japanese Zen painters used the term *wabi* to define the "unfashionable poverty" of their bare, intentionally non-symmetrical and "imperfect" representations. Using fast, dry brushstrokes, they painted with inspired connectedness to the phenomenal world, thus conveying both the transient vividness of "things as they are" and their own expression of Buddhist "suchness".

Japanese Zen painters also redefined the landscape tradition with their own delicately stylized natural scenes. The immensity of the Chinese mountain panorama, which traditionally represented spiritual exaltation, gave way to studies of pines, rock, bamboo and orchids – views that were smaller in scale, but embodied a vision of Buddhist totality.

Zen literature

Teachers often differed on the subject of Zen doctrine. The more orthodox relied on texts, while others, basing their practice on subjective experience, worked without scripture. The Japanese master Dōgen worked skilfully within both traditions. Dōgen's own works, ranging from practical monastic instruction to profound poetic metaphysics, are canonical in Zen literature, and Dōgen was also the first Japanese teacher to deliver informal lectures, many of which are contained in his book of essays, *Shobogenzo* (*Treasury of the Eye of the True Dharma*).

In the heat haze
single-petalled poppies
shimmer.
KATO KYŌTAI

_____

Zen meditation.
Blood-gorged
mosquitoes.
TAN TAIGI

釣鐘に
とカリて
光る

蛍の示

A firefly

has alighted on the temple bell,

and glitters.

SHIKI

Meditation

The classic account of Buddhist meditation is contained in an early Indian text called the *Satipatthana Sutta* (*Development of Awareness Discourse*). The Buddha outlines how a monk should seek out a remote place, adopt an upright posture, regulate the breath and then fix the attention on breathing until the mind is concentrated. By this means tranquillity and awareness grow, and in the mind space opens in which the Buddha's teaching can be comprehended and internalized, leading to profound insight.

Zen meditation as taught by Japanese masters followed largely the same practice. When the 12th-century Japanese master Dōgen studied in China, his master Hongzhi advised him to meditate sitting "in silent introspection without confusion from inner thoughts of grasping …" From this practice of self-reliant passivity, said Hongzhi, "you can return to deal with events."

"Monks," Dōgen himself wrote, "should withdraw and reflect on themselves separated from human habitation, resting as with the floating clouds or running water, and pursue enlightenment." Dōgen's clouds and water also suggest the changes in nature that demonstrate the impermanence of all things, comprehension of which was a constituent of enlightenment. "You can see that moments pass without stopping, and that all is transient," wrote Dōgen: "Use each fleeting moment." Using the moment also means not wasting our brief human existence pursuing fame, profit or pleasure. To meditate was urgent. "Now," Dōgen wrote in a famous discourse, "is the time to save your head from a scorching fire" – the fire of attachment to the world, to sensory experiences, and to delusions of self.

Koans

S tudents of the Japanese Rinzai school focus their
meditation on *koans* – riddles, paradoxical sayings and
stories from the lives and conversations of Zen masters – to
help them to break through into *satori* (enlightenment). The
purpose of a *koan* is to transcend conventional thought with a
problem that is impossible to solve logically, such as "What
face did you have before you were born?"

Koans form part of a Zen monastic training that includes
other unorthodox and sometimes non-verbal approaches. To
"open new areas of vision", as Zen master Ma Tsu exppressed
it, a teacher might strike or shout at a student, or simply walk
away, to shock the questioner into first-hand apprehension
of a reality that cannot be described or explained. One
master compared such teaching to "pushing someone off
a 10,000-foot cliff". In thus "losing his life", the "victim"
shed the ignorance that separated him from enlightenment.

The beautiful and disconcerting conversations of the
Chinese sages were collected into several Zen anthologies,
and these were translated into Japanese and systematized by
Rinzai teachers. One such collection, the *Mumonkan* (*The
Gateless Gate*), compares its *koans* to a tangled wisteria vine.

If I opened the door
I could show all the buddhas
the spring blossom.

KAAI CHIGETSU

From the nose
of that colossal Buddha
a swallow emerges.

ISSA

露

露のせを
つゆをながら
さり
かうら

The world is a dewdrop,
a dewdrop world …
it is, it is, it is what is …
Issa

Suffering

At the centre of the Buddha's teaching were the Four Noble Truths, which start very simply with the fact that all people suffer, and the cause of this suffering is desire. The third truth lay in the Buddha's realization that he could, as a "physician" to humankind, prescribe a way out of our suffering. In the fourth truth the Buddha outlined the Middle Way of morality and meditation that leads to liberation.

These teachings formed the basis of all later Buddhist thought, and few teachers have denied the reality of suffering. Only the perfectly enlightened might claim immunity from at least some psychological misery, and many Buddhist teachers and writers have been helpfully honest about their own experience of sorrow.

From as early as the tenth century, Japanese poets in fact dedicated themselves to expressing the relationship between beauty and sadness, and to identifying *aware* (sorrow) all around them. Bashō was so candid about his feelings that on many occasions he described how he stopped to weep, his tears falling in harmony with a sorrow he perceives in nature and in the passage of time. Parting from friends, the poet is blinded by tears, and, as he puts it in a characteristic haiku,

his sorrow is shared by birds and fish, who also lament the passing of the spring season.

The 19th-century poet Issa was also preoccupied with both his own suffering and the misery he saw around him. In one passage Issa, himself a Buddhist priest, described the accidental drowning of a young boy on a herb-gathering expedition. "His parents wept bitterly in everybody's view. They were Buddhist priests who taught indifference to suffering. But who could blame them?"

Transience

S uffering, impermanence and not-self: these are the Three Characteristics by which the Buddha defined human existence. According to the Buddha, failure to accept the transience of life leads to suffering. "All phenomena are subject to decay," the Buddha serenely told his grieving monks as he prepared for his own death. Legend has it that two great sal trees withered at this moment.

Japanese classical literature is suffused with a sense of transience. In part this reveals the influence of Buddhist ideas, in part it expresses a melancholic reflection on human life and the natural cycle of growth and decay. Ordinary existence, to Japanese Buddhists, was *ukiyo* (the floating world), ultimately unreal and as impermanent as a dewdrop. The final part of Lady Murasaki's *The Tale of Genji* is called *The Bridge of Dreams*: a title intended to describe life itself. In Murasaki's 11th-century Japan, even Buddhism was believed to be in its decadent, latter days. The opening of the *Tale of the Heike*, a 12th-century novel about the wars that shattered the tranquil Heian period (see pages 32–3), proclaims the same message: "The bell of the Gion Temple rings to warn every man that everything is vanity and evanescence."

Pilgrimage

V isits to sites connected with the lives of spiritual teachers are a part of most religions. Before his death, the Buddha enjoined his followers to make pilgrimages to key places in his life, including the site of his enlightenment at Bodh Gaya and the deer park at Sarnath where he delivered his first sermon. People began to make Buddhist pilgrimages in Japan soon after the religion arrived from China in the sixth century. But many of these journeys took place alongside Shinto pilgrimages.

Sarashina Nikki, the 11th-century diary of Lady Sarashina (see page 52), describes visits to both Buddhist and Shinto shrines within a single evening. While Shinto devotions would be undertaken to ensure purity and health, a Buddhist would hope to secure good karma, and would see pilgrimages as a way of ensuring a fortunate rebirth by accumulating "merit". This they achieved by undertaking difficult journeys to remote country temples and by praying, fasting and reciting Buddhist *sutras* at shrines to saints and teachers.

Such pilgrimages were lonely, and could be dangerous as there were often bandits on the roads. As a result, Kyoto's educated classes during Lady Sarashina's time tended to prefer

the comfort and excitement of the urban ceremonial cycle.
On one occasion Lady Sarashina left Kyoto during a rare
Shinto ritual. Her brother ridiculed her and warned that she
would be laughed at for generations. But others argued that
to stay and watch the ceremony was mere sightseeing, while
genuine pilgrims would gain the Buddha's favour. Many
pilgrims gave their journeys added meaning by writing poems
at significant places – many of Sarashina's poems survive.

Above: Memorial tablets stand near a Shinto shrine on Mount Haguro on Honshu Island (see page 77).

Cool, cool evening.

White moon.

Autumn wind blowing.

UEJIMA ONITSURA

_____

Wind in autumn.

For me there are no gods.

And no Buddhas.

SHIKI

松

倚朝顔　幾死苑に返る　活れ松

Priests … Morning glories …

how many have died and been reborn

beneath this pine tree?

BASHŌ

Nature

Reverence for magnificent landscape is central to Japanese culture, but everyday wonders such as animals, insects, grass and the wind could also inspire poetic reverie. *Kigo* (season words) such as "moon", "plum blossom", "rice seedling" or "firefly" are traditionally a feature of haiku poetry. The chosen *kigo* is intended to evoke all the feelings that the reader would associate with a particular season.

Reeds and rushes line the shore of one of the five lakes surrounding Mount Fuji.

Beauty and the landscape

A Japanese "landscape" painting may not represent a real landscape at all, but a setting from literature, a devotion or meditation, a city scene or an idealized – or even wholly imaginary – place. There has never been a time when a single guiding concept defined what a Japanese landscape painting "meant", in the way that it has in the West – for example, in the Romantic era, when a painted landscape was intended to inspire a sense of the sublime.

As with many aspects of Japanese culture, the earliest styles of Japanese painting were strongly influenced by Chinese traditions. In the ninth century *yamato-e* – literally "Japanese painting" – was developed at the Heian court. *Yamato-e* was closely connected to *waka* poetry (see page 16), and focused on the seasons, leading to so-called *shiki-e* (four-season artworks), which are four-panelled paintings or *byobu* (folding screens) that chart the season's progression in successive "frames". Also at this time, *meisho-e* (paintings of famous places) became popular. From Heian times, the Japanese have enjoyed ranking places, including gardens, seascapes and views, according to their beauty, and such accolades are still mentioned in guidebooks today.

Opposite: This 19th-century woodblock print by Hiroshige shows maple trees framing a view of Tekona Shrine at Mama, about ten miles east of Edo (Tokyo). The shrine is surrounded by a lake, and commemorates Tekona, a beautiful maiden who drowned herself in the lake to escape the rivalries of her many suitors.

It was not choice so much as necessity that led painters to include urban settings, imaginary features or motifs such as plants and animals in "landscape" painting. The geography of the country – a long, narrow and extremely mountainous chain of islands – made extensive travel virtually impossible, even for the very wealthy. Artists were simply drawing upon familiar surroundings in creating their scenes.

The Kanō School was particularly influential in the development of Japanese painting. Employed by a succession of Japan's shoguns from Oda Nobunaga (1534–82) onward, painters such as Kanō Eitoku adorned the interiors of castles, palaces and fortressses with highly decorative and richly coloured images of birds, flowers and trees.

Paintings from the 15th and 16th centuries show that artists were beginning to observe landscape more closely, but it was the period of the Tokugawa peace (1603–1868) that decisively transformed the way that Japanese landscape was appreciated and depicted. With peace came commerce, and a series of great highways across Japan. As the merchant classes prospered, so did the rest of society, and increased income and leisure made it possible for even the lower classes to travel.

Mount Fuji

The highest mountain in Japan stands on Honshu, the largest island in the Japanese archipelago. Mount Fuji is classified as an active volcano, though an eruption has not occurred since 1707. The mountain has been regarded as sacred for thousands of years and is a Shinto holy place, where *kami* are believed to reside. It has also been widely celebrated in literature and art. Women were forbidden to climb the mountain until the Meiji era. Today more than 300,000 people reach the summit every year.

By the 18th century *ukiyo-e* (woodblock prints) had become popular. *Ukiyo-e* (literally "pictures of the floating world") depicted the entertainment district of theatres, restaurants, teahouses and "pleasure quarters" that sprang up as Edo grew rich, as well as respectable city streets, scenic views from highway journeys, and landscapes.

Great series of *ukiyo-e* prints depicted the newly accessible scenery, such as Andō Hiroshige's *The 53 Stations of the Tokaido Road*. The *meisho* (famous places) formerly only imagined in literature were now stopping-points for the cultivated traveller, and again Hiroshige was there, producing his *Famous Views of the 60-odd Provinces*.

But old traditions did not die out. As literacy spread and high culture filtered down the social classes, literature that had inspired the court painters of an earlier age, such as the tenth-century *Ise Monogatari* (*Tales of Ise*), found a wider audience. So just as the "real thing" became accessible to Japan's travellers, *meisho-e* pictures of landscapes inspired by literature, such as the celebrated Musashino Plain, also enjoyed popularity. The real and the ideal have never been far apart in the Japanese appreciation of the natural world.

Rocks on the shore.
Lots of little plovers
run nimbly.
MUKAI KYORAI

Tangling a willow
and untangling,
the wind blows.
CHIYOJO

春人海
終日乃るり
のたり哉

The sea in spring time –
all day rising, falling,
rising, falling.
BUSON

Shinto shrines

S hinto's gods, known as *kami*, are the spirits of nature, the seasons and the agricultural cycle. Its first holy places, therefore, were not built structures but sacred spaces centred on naturally occurring features such as rocks, trees, caves and waterfalls, often with simple stone altars on which offerings to the *kami* were laid.

Straw ropes known as *shimenawa*, decorated with zigzags of folded white paper called *gohei*, were (and still are) hung on sacred trees, rocks, buildings and shrine gates to indicate holy space. The area surrounded by *shimenawa* was known as *himorogi* if the *kami* was that of a tree, or *iwasaka* if the spirit belonged to a rock, and rites were performed inside it.

When Buddhism was introduced from China in the sixth century, Shinto shrines began to change under its influence. In imitation of this new creed which worshipped an image of the Buddha housed in a temple hall, *honden* (sanctuaries) were built to house the *kami*, and these were then enclosed by spectacular *haiden* (halls of worship) at traditional holy sites.

Today a visitor to a Shinto shrine first passes through a *torii* (sacred gateway). Every shrine has a trough of pure water, where worshippers wash their hands and mouths before

Ise shrine

Japan's supreme Shinto shrine, Ise, is famous for its quasi-mythical renewal ritual. Phoenix-like, it is destroyed then rebuilt every 20 years – a rite performed faithfully since 690. Dedicated to the sun goddess Amaterasu, Ise shrine exists in two places at once. Every 20 years a new shrine is built alongside the old one, and the old one is pulled down. The site of the old shrine is marked with white pebbles, until its turn comes again 20 years later. The 62nd rebuilding will take place in 2013.

Opposite: *Gohei* (folded white paper) hangs from a sacred tree.

approaching the altar. They then stand silently in awe within the divine presence.

Kami are also still worshipped in the open, with few or no built structures around them – Mount Fuji is a celebrated Shinto holy place, and though the sacred island of Miyajima hosts numerous shrine and temple buildings, its most famous symbol is the so-called "floating *torii*", a red lacquered arch that stands in the waters offshore.

Japan's national sport, sumo, began as a ritual display of strength performed at Shinto shrines for the entertainment of the *kami*. The clay and sand *dhoyō* (rings) are ritually purified with salt, and taboos apply – including the prohibition of women. *Shimenawa* are also worn during sumo rituals by *yokozuna*, sumo's highest-ranked wrestlers.

The most celebrated Shinto shrines in Japan are Tokyo's Meiji Jingu and Kyoto's Heian Jingu, both imperial shrines (as indicated by the use of the word *jingu* rather than *jinja* for shrine); Kamakura's Tsurugaoka Hachimangu, dedicated to Hachiman, the *kami* of war; the Toshogu Shrine at Nikkō, sacred to the powerful Tokugawa clan; and Ise shrine (see page 111), dedicated to Amaterasu.

Opposite: The *torii* of Itsukushima shrine off Miyajima Island at sunset. It is the largest Shinto *torii* in Japan. Many of the shrine buildings are also built on the water. Traditionally, worshippers were not permitted on to the sacred island itself: instead they approached by boat, passing first through the *torii*.

A young woman
planting seedlings
plants toward her crying baby.
TAKARAI KIKAKU

———————————————

How art begins:
a rice-planting song
in the deep interior.
BASHŌ

花

花にきて
もにいねぶる
ひとま家

Coming to view cherry blossom,
I lie beneath the flowering branches
and sleep.
BUSON

The cycle of the seasons

J apan enjoys four distinct seasons that have inspired native artists and poets down the centuries and are still a source of pride to Japanese today.

Many social rituals mark the passing of the seasons, from spring's *hanami* (flower watching) to September's *tsukimi* (moon watching) and the *koyo* (red leaves) of October and November. These have been the occasion for merry-making since Heian times, and are enjoyed to this day – many Japanese will travel to celebrated beauty spots, especially around Kyoto, for a weekend's autumn leaf viewing.

These seasonal social observations provide the setting for many great works of classical Japanese literature, among them Sei Shonagon's *Pillow Book* and Lady Murasaki's *The Tale of Genji*. Indeed, literature was often composed at seasonal parties. Sometimes poems would be floated down a river in a winecup: if the party were by a lake, the challenge would be to compose a poem in the time it took one's cup, floated out on the waters, to sink.

Haiku, of course, is the literary form most closely tied to the seasons. *Kigo* (season words) are an essential component of any traditional haiku, and many haiku focus on the weather

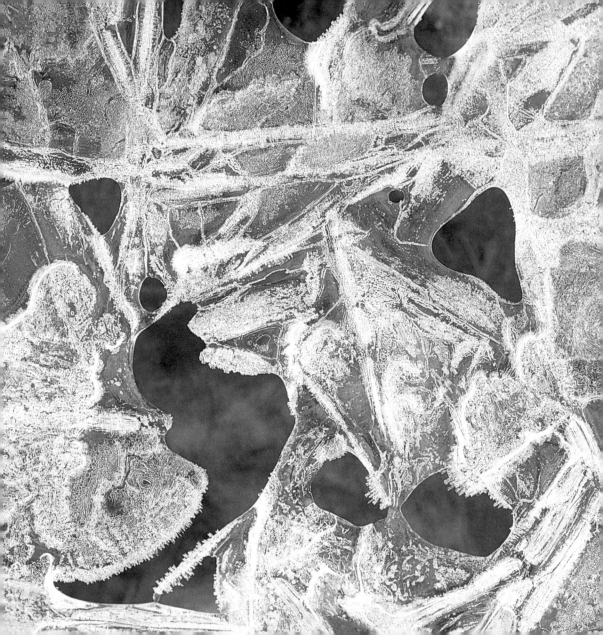

and seasonal experiences. *Kigo* can be remarkably precise in their reference to seasonal phenomena – spring weather *kigo*, for example, include *tsuchifuru* (yellow dust), blown from China during the springtime, while early winter is suggested by *kogarashi* – literally a "tree-withering wind".

Seasonal subjects are also enduringly popular in Japanese visual arts. As with *kigo*, certain flowers are associated with particular seasons, so a flower may appear as a single artwork symbolizing a season, or as a seasonal detail in a complex image. Among the most popular are *sakura* (cherry) for spring; *ajisai* (hydrangea) for summer; *kiku* (chrysanthemum) for autumn; and the wintry *ume* (plum) and *tsubaki* (camellia).

One ancient custom that has survived to this day, despite Japan's extensive urbanization in the past 50 years, is the exchange of gifts of seasonal food, usually fruits: cherries in early summer; watermelon, which are smashed with a stick in a popular summer game; peach, persimmon and grapes in autumn; and citrus fruits in winter, especially the native *mikan* (tangerine) and lemon-like *yuzu*. These gifts bring even the modern Tokyoite in touch with the cycle of the seasons that dominated the lives of his or her farming forebears.

Categories of *kigo*

Every haiku poet's best friend is a *saijiki*, the dictionary of *kigo*. Words for each season are subdivided into seven categories. Two relate to the social world (events and daily life); the other five belong to the natural world: plants, animals, the heavens (celestial bodies, storms, light and shade), the earth (mountains, forests, lakes, river, the sea), and the season (temperature, weather, length of days).

Opposite: A huge wave towers over a diminutive view of Mount Fuji in this woodblock print by Hokusai. The boats are thought to be barges carrying fish to the markets in Edo (Tokyo).

Cherry blossom

Japan's admiration of the cherry tree goes back as far as its recorded culture, but it is the cherry blossom, of course, that is most famously celebrated. From the classical Heian period to this day, friends and co-workers gather for *hanami* parties to admire the flowers and eat, drink and make merry – often, these days, with karaoke. Today the best spots are staked out with a blue tarpaulin, and companies may send a junior worker to sit in a park or temple grounds all day to guard their place.

The appeal of cherry blossom to the Japanese sensibility is twofold. It heralds the beginning of spring and therefore the rebirth of the year, and an abundant blossoming is said to promise a rich harvest. However, the pale blossoms usually last less than a week, and their brief flowering and inevitable fall bring to mind the precarious nature of life and the certainty of its passing.

It is for this latter quality that the cherry was prized by the Heian courtiers of classical Japan, with their love of *mono no aware*, the "pathos of things". Heian *hanami* parties would feature poetry-writing contests, and *sakura* (cherry) is a haiku *kigo* (season word) used to evoke springtime.

The warriors' flower

Cherished by poets, cherry blossom was transformed into an emblem of warriors with the emergence of the samurai class: the flower became the symbol of *bushidō*, the "way of the warrior". The samurai ideal was to fall, like the blossom, at the height of his glory; cherry petals fall to the ground quickly rather than floating, used to symbolize a non-attachment to life and a direct approach to death that was much admired in Japanese chivalry. Cherry blossom more recently became the symbol of the *kamikaze* suicide pilots in World War II.

Bird on the water.

Looks so heavy,

floating.

UEJIMA ONITSURA

―――――――――――

I thought those birds

were leaves

in the winter moonlight.

CHIYOJO

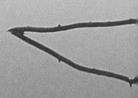

夕月

海くれて
鴨の声
ほのかに白し

The darkening sea.
A wild duck calls –
in a blur of whiteness.

BASHŌ

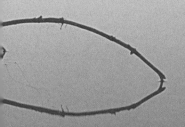

Festivals

J apan's festival year is a crowded one, and many events are as enthusiastically observed as they were centuries ago. There are two annual festival periods: *O-shōgatsu*, the New Year, and *O-bon*, the summertime festival of the dead. Additionally, various one-day celebrations fall throughout the year, including *Seijin-shiki* (Coming-of-Age Day, January), *Hinamatsuri* (Doll's Festival, March), *Tanabata* (Star Festival, July), and *Shichi-Go-San* (Seven-Five-Three, November).

In addition to the calendar and seasonal festivals, many shrines and temples mark *matsuri* (festival days) of their own, most commonly during the *O-bon* period. There is rarely much religious pomp or ceremony involved. Booths along the approach to the shrine or temple sell *matsuri* food or host children's games such as scooping for goldfish. If the shrine compound has a stage, it will be used for classical music and dance, as has been traditional for centuries.

Larger shrine festivals involve the spectacular carrying of *mikoshi* (portable shrines), which resemble highly decorated, veiled sedan-chairs that hold a god, the shrine deity, rather than a person. The hidden god is paraded through the streets before being returned to the shrine.

Fighting shrines

Kenka mikoshi (fighting shrines) are among the most spectacular of Shinto celebrations. The portable shrines are carried by teams of young men from neighbouring city districts or villages, who ram rival shrines or attack them with bamboo spears. The shrines will often "fight" until one of them is destroyed.

Opposite: Performers dance the *Shishimai* (Lion Dance) during the autumn Niwaka festival to ensure peace and good health.

Animals

Symbolism involving animals is entrenched in Japanese life thanks to the 12-animal Chinese zodiac. People are believed to share characteristics with their birth-year animal, and calendar years are said to reflect their given animal: rabbit years thus portend sociability, harmony and opportunity.

Japanese folklore and religion are overrun with animals. Instead of a man's face, when Japanese look at the moon they see a rabbit on its hind legs pounding *mochi* rice cakes – a classical poetic term for the moon was *gyokuto* (jewelled hare). Shinto shrines are guarded by *kitsune* (foxes) – besides being the messengers of Inari Myojin, the god of agriculture, *kitsune* are the most celebrated tricksters of Japanese folklore.

Japan has also inherited classical Chinese animal symbols: cranes for longevity, mandarin ducks for marital fidelity (often embroidered on wedding kimonos) and turtles for safe travels. The butterfly symbolizes joy, as well as carrying religious connotations of immortality and rebirth; and butterflies may be found drawn on manuscripts or included in artwork to bring felicity. Other cherished insects are the firefly and the dragonfly, the latter being the subject of Japan's best-loved children's song, "Aka Tonbo" (Red Dragonfly).

Drinker's friend

A favourite mythical mischief-maker is the *tanuki* (raccoon-dog). Like the *kitsune*, the *tanuki* is a shape-shifter, but he is also the guardian of drunkards and gluttons. To this day, many restaurants and liquor stores have a *tanuki* statue at the door – identified by the sake flask held in one paw and the account book in the other, a warning that pleasure may prove dearly bought.

Firefly

on my hand

fades sadly.

MUKAI KYORAI

_____

On the face of the sea

a swallow

has erased a rainbow.

TAKARAI KIKAKU

蝸牛

蝸牛そろそろ
登枇
冨士の山

The snail climbs
Mount Fuji
slowly, slowly …
ISSA

Arts and Culture

Long traditions, precise rules and expert craftsmanship governed the production of Japanese creative arts. Visual representation, including calligraphy, *sumi-e* ink painting and *ukiyo-e* prints, reached levels of transcendent beauty, whilst religious ritual, meditation and intricate skill informed the practice of tea ceremony and the design of Japanese and Zen gardens.

The eighth-century poet Nakamaro, exiled in China, gazes at the moon knowing that the same moon shines over Japan, in this 19th-century print by Hokusai.

Calligraphy

T he beauty of *shodo* (calligraphy) is hard-won. The Japanese themselves regard it as the greatest achievement of the dazzling Heian period.

For millennia Japan was culturally sophisticated, but lacked a written language. In the sixth century the great Prince Shōtoku (see page 24) instigated a move to adopt a writing system to record such essentials as military instructions, history and poetry, and the Japanese, as was their custom in matters of cultural self-improvement, borrowed directly from China.

However, Chinese was linguistically a poor match for the shape and texture of the Japanese language. After three centuries of trying to write using only difficult Chinese *kanji* characters, the Japanese started to innovate. The ninth century saw the advent of two phonetic syllable "alphabets": angular *katakana*, used at first for official documents and Buddhist *sutras*, and cursive *hiragana*. Japanese has kept the same three written forms ever since.

By the 11th century *hiragana* was used for *waka* poetry and personal writings, and it was *hiragana*,

the simplest and most graceful of the three styles, that came to epitomize all that is most beautiful in Japanese calligraphy. Because it was not regarded as seemly for women to read or write Chinese, *hiragana* became known as *onnade* (woman's hand). It was the script used by the celebrated Heian female authors Sei Shonagon and Lady Murasaki.

The artistic height of *onnade* is the graceful, flowing, yet dynamic *masu-shikishi* calligraphy. This achieves a kind of synergy between the sense and appearance of words, with syllable-characters elongated or compressed, or even words broken over columns, to create a cohesive visual whole.

Calligraphy was also used for pleasure (Heian aristocrats would throw calligraphy parties) and for reflection – the copying of *sutras* was regarded as a form of meditation. Skill at calligraphy is still considered to reveal a refined personality.

The concept of beauty in Japanese calligraphy is governed by strict definitions. For example, every piece of work must have at least one *nijimi* (blotted) and one *kasure* (patchy) area. Today there are three recognized calligraphic styles: *kaisho* (square), *gyosho* (semi-cursive) and *sosho* (cursive). *Sosho* most closely resembles the fluid Heian ideal.

Opposite: A courtesan practises calligraphy in this print from 18th-century Edo. Along with skill in music, tea ceremony, dance, poetry and conversation, calligraphy was considered a key accomplishment for the women of the pleasure quarters. The calligraphy above the courtesan's head is made up of both *hiragana* (the simpler, cursive characters) and *kanji* (the more complex characters) – a mixture that is commonly used in Japan today.

Ink painting

The spare black-and-white style of *sumi-e* (ink picture) painting was developed in China during the Sung Dynasty (960-1274) and brought to Japan by Buddhist monks in the early decades of the Muromachi period (1338-1573). *Sumi-e*, also known as *suibokuga* (water-ink-picture), was initially practised as an aid to meditation, expressing the spiritual insight and energy of Buddhist thought.

Sumi-e are always monochrome. It was widely held that painting in only black and white was more demanding than painting with a full palette of colour. The blank, white space of the paper is an integral part of the composition, balancing the black ink in a yin-yang dualism.

As with colour and composition, so with technique: simplicity is all. There are four basic strokes in *sumi-e* painting: the Bamboo, the Wild Orchid, the Chrysanthemum and the Plum Branch. Known as the "Four Gentlemen" or "Four Friends", these strokes symbolize various ideals. The evergreen bamboo is sturdy yet supple; the rare orchid is elegant yet retiring; the chrysanthemum is contemplative, a late flower, appearing just before winter; while the plum tree blossoms in winter and its flowers drop before they wither.

Wordlessness

The Buddha once preached a "wordless sermon", in which he silently stepped forward, picked up a flower, put it down again and returned to his place. Everyone was baffled, save for the disciple Mahakasyapa, who understood the Buddha's meaning. In the same way, the white space of a *sumi-e* or what is unsaid in haiku – the "wordless line" – conveys as much as, if not more than, what is set to paper.

Opposite: *Sumi-e* can be seen as a form of visual haiku. Highly impressionistic, it captures the essence of its subject in the fewest strokes possible.

Ukiyo-e prints

D espite their high standing with modern art lovers, the coloured woodblock prints known as *ukiyo-e* began as a bourgeois art form of the 18th century, mass-produced for the newly affluent classes of Japan's expanding capital city, Edo (Tokyo). When *ukiyo-e* first arrived in Europe, they were often used as wrapping paper.

Mokuhanga (woodblock printing) was a traditional Japanese art form, but its output was monochrome, with hand-coloured tints of reddish orange. The technique developed rapidly in the second half of the 18th century with the introduction of an expensive Chinese method of multiblock printing, which enabled printers to use multiple colours.

The first accomplished examples of Japanese multicoloured woodblock art were the *nishki-e* (brocade prints), produced by Harunobu Suzuki in the 1760s and 1770s. Just a few decades later came the great flowering of *ukiyo-e*. Three names stand out: Kitagawa Utamaro (1754–1806), Katsushika Hokusai (1760–1849) and Andō Hiroshige (1797–1858).

Utamaro was the first great artist of the genre and his subjects epitomize the "floating world". Loose-limbed courtesans were captured during their sensual assignations or

Ukiyo-e and *Japonisme*

Just as haiku influenced a generation of Western poets including Ezra Pound, *ukiyo-e* prints had a lasting effect on the perceptions of Western artists. Claude Monet's house at Giverny is filled with the artist's collection of *ukiyo-e*, while Vincent van Gogh wrote in 1887:"I envy the Japanese artists for the incredible neat clarity of all their works … as simple as breathing."

Opposite: In this print by Hokusai, pilgrims admire Mount Fuji from a tower attached to the Five-Hundred-Rakan Temple in Edo. This would have been the highest point in the city, the ideal vantage point for a spectacular view.

in casual domestic moments – washing, mending or smoking pipes. Hokusai created the famous *Aka Fuji* (*Red Fuji*), an iconic picture of Japan's emblematic mountain glowing red against a blue cloud-strewn sky. Hiroshige's work is lyrical and often has the format of a travelogue.

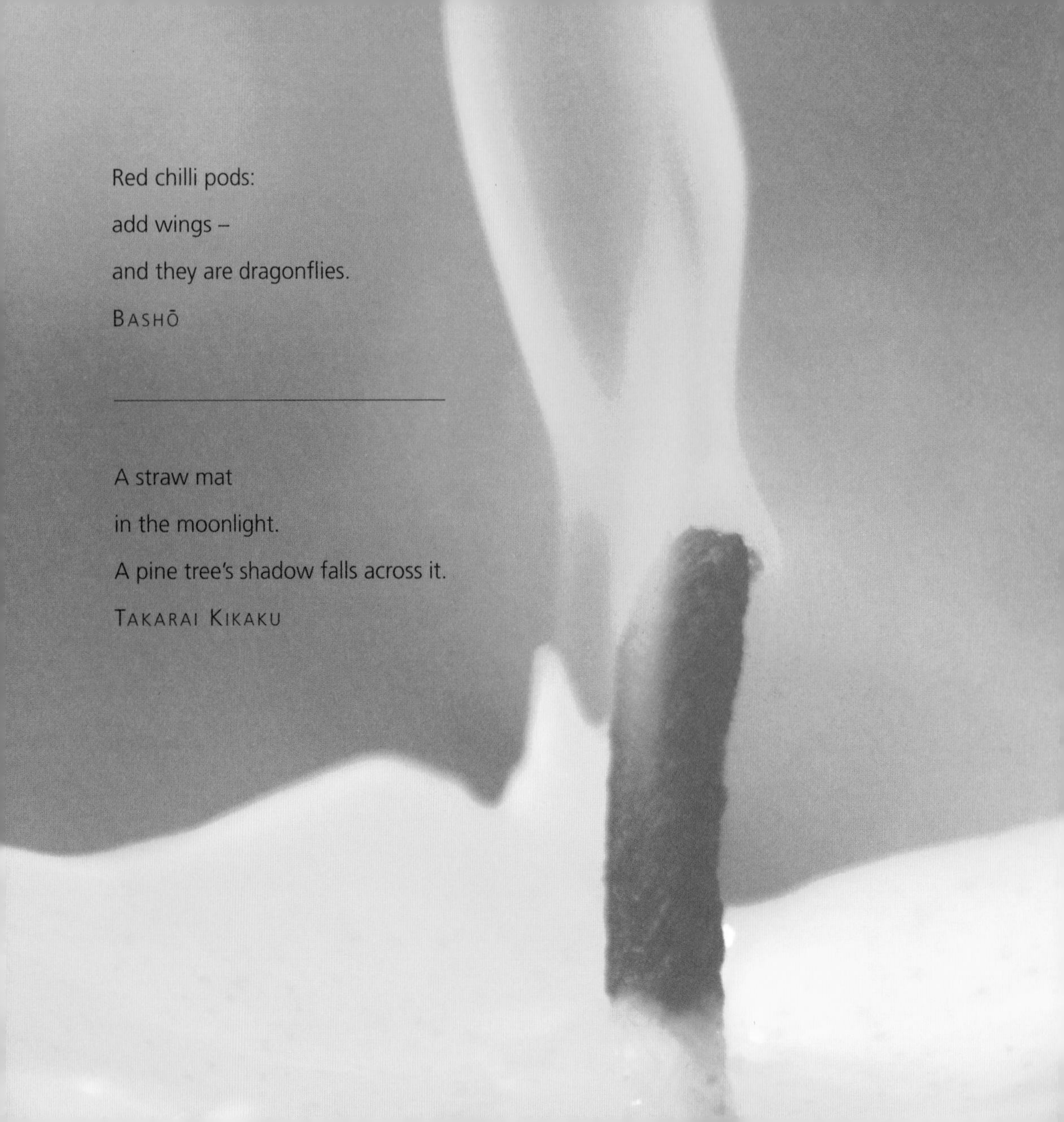

Red chilli pods:

add wings –

and they are dragonflies.

BASHŌ

―――――――――――――――

A straw mat

in the moonlight.

A pine tree's shadow falls across it.

TAKARAI KIKAKU

花火

人帰る
花火の後の
暗きかな

Everyone's gone home.
The fireworks are over.
How dark the night is!
SHIKI

Japanese gardens

L ike many other forms of artistic expression, the Japanese garden was a cultural import from China that underwent rapid transformation into a distinctive aesthetic. The oldest gardening manual in the world is Japanese: *Sakuteiki* (*The Book of Garden Making*) was written 1,000 years ago. Gardens created centuries ago according to its directions can still be seen, and its precepts are still followed today.

One distinctive style of garden that arose after the *Sakuteiki* was the paradise garden, designed to recreate the "Pure Land" of the Amida Buddha. Whereas the Christian Garden of Eden is a place of lush abundance, riotous with flowers and fruit, the Buddhist paradise is a place of contemplative stillness. Water is essential to this "reflective" process, an idea that led to the *shinden* garden, which contains a corridor of linked buildings on the edge of a southerly pond. Visitors would view such gardens from a boat.

An enduring principle in *Sakuteiki* is *shakkei* (borrowed scenery). Referring to the landscape that is visible beyond the realms of the garden, this "borrowed scenery" is more than an attractive backdrop. Plants or trees are arranged so as to draw the viewer's eye up to, for example, a distant mountain.

Opposite: This garden in San Francisco showcases many of the key features of the Japanese garden aesthetic. The pathways provide a variety of perspectives for the visitor – low over the water, high up on the bridge – and the water itself is integrated closely with the plants, trees and mossy rocks, and the architecture of the garden space.

Zen gardens

No garden style in the world is as distinctive as the Japanese Zen garden. But there are actually several kinds of Zen garden, each capturing some aspect of the elusive, tranquil spirit of this sect of Buddhism.

Karesansui (dry–rock–and–water) are the most celebrated Zen gardens. With their wavy gravel and jutting rocks, they create a fantastical seascape of mountains and islands. Raking the gravel is a daily contemplative ritual for the monks.

Kyoto is home to a celebrated example of another type of Zen garden. Saiho-ji has earned the nickname *Koke-dera* (moss temple) for its garden of 100 types of moss. The garden is admired for the collaboration between man and nature that allows the slow-growing mosses to thrive undisturbed.

Even the stroll garden, which found popularity among the nobility in the 17th century as they appropriated ever larger areas of land, was essentially spiritual in concept. This type of garden was born in India, where the devout used their walk to symbolize a journey through the spiritual centre of the Buddhist universe. The continually shifting perspectives encourage the visitor to slow down and view the world from different angles.

Symbol and effect

The most famous Zen garden is Ryoanji in Kyoto, which features 15 rocks arranged in five groups. It is suggestive of a seascape, and in the simple arrangement people have seen a tigress crossing the waters with cubs, and an allusion to the Chinese character for "heart". Researchers at the University of Kyoto recently claimed that the spaces between the rocks formed a pattern of spreading tree branches – the source of its soothing effect.

Opposite: Carefully raked gravel in a Zen garden aids contemplation and instils a feeling of serenity.

Tea ceremony

Despite the fact that tea ceremony is arguably the most famous of all Japan's arts, *cha* (tea) is not native to the archipelago. Although the date of tea's arrival from China is still debated, records suggest that tea was first served in Japan by the Emperor Shomu (724–49) as he entertained Buddhist monks. Whenever tea first reached Japan's shores, it was almost certainly a monk who brought it, as tea was originally drunk in monasteries to help monks to stay awake during the long, silent hours of meditation. The beverage was also regarded as medicinal – a claim supported by modern science.

We know that the fine-quality strain of tea that has since become associated with *cha-no-yu* (the Art of Tea) arrived in Japan in 1191. The seeds were carried from China by the monk Eisai, who is also credited with introducing *matcha*, the ground, powdered form of unfermented green leaf tea. Tea ceremonies during those early centuries were the opposite of the stripped-down refinement of the *cha-no-yu* practised today. The 13th century saw a craze for *tocha* – a guessing game in which participants had to identify the origins of up to 100 bowls of tea. Among the wealthy, tea was drunk at lavish parties, with ostentatious utensils.

The art of tea

Although refined simplicity is at the heart of the tea ceremony ideal, the conduct of the ceremony itself is remarkably complex. Guests enter the tea house through a tiny entrance (27 × 31in/ 70 × 80cm), and kneel in silence on *tatami* mats facing the *furo* (brazier). The host enters and cleans the tea implements in turn. He then prepares the tea using a bowl, ground green tea, a bamboo dipper for hot water and a bamboo whisk. Each guest drinks from the bowl in turn, taking care to admire the bowl as well as the tea.

Two men revolutionized the ritual of tea. Murata Shuko (1422-1502) pioneered the humble tea room, just four-and-a-half *tatami* mats large (approximately 8 × 8ft/2.5 × 2.5m square), and the practice of preparing the tea in front of his aristocratic guests. Shuko also began the tradition of using exquisitely crafted Japanese utensils to serve tea.

It is the name of Sen-no-Rikyū (1522-91), however, that is synonymous with tea ceremony and *chado* (the Way of Tea). Although a wealthy merchant's son, Rikyū was inspired by the simplicity with which monks prepared their tea. He applied those Zen principles to the secular practice of tea ceremony, and devised a profoundly influential aesthetic, *wabi* (desolation), a kind of stark rustic beauty.

Four principles guide Sen-no-Rikyū's *wabi-cha* (*wabi*-style tea); *wa* (harmony), the defining concept of Japanese society; *kei* (respect and reverence); *sei* (purity), a concept derived from Shinto ritual; and *jaku* (tranquillity). Rikyū's ideal was to create the perfect setting in which to enjoy a bowl of tea and to capture the fleeting spirit of the occasion. Most eminent tea practitioners in Japan today belong to one of two schools, both founded by great-grandsons of Rikyū.

Music and dance

Japan's classical music is the least well-known of all its traditional arts. While *kabuki* theatre, haiku poetry and *ukiyo-e* prints are famous around the world, *gagaku* (courtly music) and its instruments are less familiar. But not only is *gagaku* hauntingly beautiful, it is also closely intertwined with the development of *bugaku* (Japanese dance) and poetry. The word *uta*, for example, is used for both "poem" and "song". And from this blend of music, poetry and dance came Japan's renowned theatrical forms, *noh* and *kabuki* (see pages 150–1).

Gagaku and *bugaku* developed in the Nara (710–94) and Heian periods. Today the sounds of the lute-like *biwa*, the recumbent, 13-stringed *koto* and the 17-pipe mouth organ *sho* – said to sound like the human voice – can plunge a listener back into the golden age of Japanese creativity. To Western ears, the music often sounds arrhythmic, almost otherworldly.

Distinct from the courtly music of *gagaku* were popular regional ballads and dances, and also religious forms of music and movement. *Noh* dance-drama was directly influenced by Buddhist *shomyo*, a recitation of Buddhist sutras set to a melody, which had an element of performance. Dance was also the origin of Japan's best-known theatrical style: *kabuki*.

Dancing in the streets

Today a grand set-piece dance is at the heart of Japan's most notable festival, the August *O-bon* (see page 125). In locations ranging from remote villages to Tokyo bus depots, people are summoned by a high, piping tune and the beat of a drum. Wearing their *yukata* (cotton summer kimonos), they gather and circle a gaily decorated float on which musicians sit, and dance through the night, repeating a sequence of simple steps and gestures.

Opposite: A *ukiyo-e* print from the Kanō School, showing men and women dancing together.

Theatre

Japan has produced many celebrated theatrical forms. *Noh*, classical Japanese drama, was first recorded in 1375, when shogun Yoshimitsu Ashikaga saw a theatre performance by an actor and his 12-year-old son. The boy was Motokiyo Zeami, known today as the "father" of *noh*.

Zeami and his father would have been well-versed in two traditional entertainments: *sarugaku* (comic drama) and *dengaku* (dance and acrobatics). By the middle of the 14th century, these had coalesced into a kind of narrative dance-drama, resembling *noh*. Zeami went on to become a prolific writer of *noh* drama. His historical and mythological plays invoke the golden age of Heian Japan. An actor himself, Zeami also penned a how-to manual for aspiring *noh* actors: *Kakyo* (*A Mirror Held to a Flower*), still used today.

Kabuki has more disreputable origins. At the dawn of the 17th century, peace was established after a period of civil war, and Japan was parched of entertainment. A dancer named Okuni took her troupe of girls to the dry bed of the Kamo River in Kyoto – a popular spot, often used by the local "teahouses" to showcase their courtesans – where they performed characterful dances, many of which required

Opposite: A *kabuki* actor in the role of celebrated samurai Fuwa Banzaemon. In *kabuki* drama he is the deadly rival of fellow samurai Nagoya Sanza – many plays revolve around their attempts to win the favours of the same courtesan, Katsuruagi. Banzaemon's kimono is covered with a distinctive "lightning in the clouds" pattern.

Okuni to don male dress. Okuni was a hit. Her dance was named *kabuki odori* (kabuki dance), from which developed a narrative form that in just two decades became *kabuki* drama. When, in 1628, women were banned from performing onstage, *kabuki* was taken over by all-male troupes. It remains an exclusively male genre, with actors specializing in female roles known as *onnagata* (literally, "in the shape of a woman").

Another influential theatrical form, *bunraku* (puppet theatre) was created in 1684. Also known as *ningyo-joruri* (puppets and storytelling), it shared one of *kabuki*'s great playwrights, Japan's "Shakespeare" Monzaemon Chikamatsu, creator of the *sewamono* (realistic play). Unusually, *bunraku* originated in mercantile Osaka, which still houses the form's National Theatre today.

Early winter.
I teach baby
to hold chopsticks.
KATO KYŌTAI

The plum blossom's here.
"Shall I steal it?"
the moon is saying.
ISSA

夕月

夕月や
梅ちり
かくる
琴乃上

Evening moon.
On the lute
plum blossom falling.
SHIKI

GLOSSARY

aware Translated as "sadness"; the quality of melancholy revered at the Heian court.

biwa Japanese lute; there are various types, but **biwa** were most commonly played with a plectrum and had four silk strings.

bunraku Puppet theatre; **bunraku** puppets have no strings.

daimyō Provincial warlords who answered to the shogun.

Edo Period, the (1600–1867) Also called the Tokugawa shogunate and the Tokugawa peace: a politically stable period during which the country was ruled by the shoguns in Tokyo; **daimyō** (warlords) ruled regionally.

geisha Name originally given to licensed female entertainers (not to be confused with courtesans) in Edo-period pleasure-quarters, who were highly skilled in arts including dance, music and tea ceremony.

gohei Zig-zag strips of white paper tied to **shimenawa** at Shinto shrines.

haibun Short prose passages, interwoven with haiku poetry.

haiga Decorative scrolls with haiku poems in calligraphy alongside appropriate **sumi-e** ink painting.

haikai no renga Informal, popular verse form that developed during the Edo period.

haiku Short three-line poem with a 5-7-5 syllable structure; key themes include nature, weather, the seasons, the loneliness of the poet and events in everyday life.

Heian period, the (794-1185) High period of Japanese courtly life and arts, centred around the imperial court in Kyoto.

hiragana Japanese syllable alphabet, characterized by its cursive flowing style; a calligraphic form of **hiragana** is called **onnade** (woman's hand).

hokku The opening verse of a **renga**, considered the most important component of the poem; its 5-7-5 structure was identical to haiku.

ikebana Japanese flower arranging, characterized by the skilful use of a few harmoniously arranged stems.

kabuki Traditional, lavishly staged theatre with popular origins; performers are heavily made-up.

Kamakura period, the (1185–1333) Era of military rule, during which the Japanese capital moved from Kyoto to Kamakura.

kampaku The regent in the imperial court; this post, along with that of **sesshu**, enabled members of the Fujiwara family to maintain control of the emperor during the Heian period (see also **sesshu**).

kanji Chinese characters adopted to write Japanese; still used today long with **katakana** and **hiragana**.

katakana Japanese syllable alphabet; this form has straighter strokes and appears more angular than **hiragana**.

makoto Translated as "sincerity", a Heian period courtly ideal.

Man'yōshū "The Collection of Many Leaves"; the oldest collection of Japanese poetry, an eighth-century anthology of poems.

Meiji era, the (1868–1912) The beginning of Japanese modernity; the emperor was restored to political power and Japan opened to the West.

mikoshi Portable Shinto shrines containing **kami**; they resemble ornate sedan chairs and are used particularly in Shinto festivals.

miyabi Translated as "courtliness"; a word used at the Heian court to denote refined courtly perfection in dress, art and personal manners.

mono no aware "The pathos of things"; an aesthetic appreciation of the sadness inherent in the world because of its impermanence.

noh Classic Japanese poetic dance-drama; the performers sometimes wear masks.

onnagata Literally "in a woman's shape", male **kabuki** actors who specialize in female roles.

renga Linked verses written by groups of poets on a theme set by the **hokku**.

sabi Poetic emotion, a kind of solitary melancholy particularly popular with wandering haiku poets.

sesshu Regent for a child emperor, a post held throughout the Heian period by members of the influential Fujiwara clan (see also **kampaku**).

shimenawa Ropes made of rice straw, used to enclose sacred Shinto space or denote holiness.

shogun Military overlords who effectively ruled Japan 1192–1867, although an emperor remained always on the throne.

sumi-e Sparse, evocative, mono-chrome ink painting, often of natural subjects and/or accompanied by calligraphy.

sutras Buddhist holy texts; believed to contain the actual words and teachings of the Buddha, although they were only written down after his death.

ukiyo Literally "the floating world"; a term used to refer the transience and ethereality of the material world.

ukiyo-e "A picture of the floating world"; a style of woodblock print produced in Japan from the 17th century onwards; notable **ukiyo-e** artists include Utamaro, Hiroshige and Hokusai.

wabi Term used for a pared-down, rustic aesthetic of imperfection, particularly important in tea ceremony ritual.

waka Poetry in the Japanese language (also called *tanka*).

yin-yang Ancient Chinese principle of balanced opposites which also influenced the development of Japanese culture; **yin** represents the cool, dark and female elements, **yang** represents the hot, bright and male.

THE POETS

Matsuo Bashō (1644–94) Widely considered the master haiku poet, Bashō is famed for both his poetry and prose, particularly the journals he wrote while on his travels around Japan. He also expressed Buddhist insights in his poetry, and was a highly respected teacher of haiku: many of his disciples became notable poets themselves.

Nozawa Bonchō (died 1714) A physicican who became an innovative follower of Bashō.

Taniguchi Buson (1715–1783) Equally skilled as a poet and painter, Buson was influenced by Bashō but developed his own vivid poetic style.

Kaai Chigetsu (*c.*1634–*c.*1708) A female haiku poet who studied with Bashō.

Chiyojo (1703–75) Japan's most celebrated female haiku poet. Her poetry expresses emotion simply, often with charm and humour.

Miura Chora (1729–80) A contemporary and associate of Buson.

Kobayashi Issa (1762–1826) Despite the tragedy and difficulty of his own personal life, Issa was an empathic, compassionate poet who had particular affinity with children and vulnerable creatures of the natural world.

Naito Jōsō (1662–1704) Originally a samurai, Jōsō became a monk after suffering ill health. He was one of Bashō's pupils.

Mukai Kyorai (1651–1704) A leading pupil of Bashō; he trained as a samurai and had great skill in martial arts.

Kato Kyōtai (1732–92) Studied haiku with Buson. He struggled to improve haiku by returning to the spirit of Bashō.

Takarai Kikaku (1661–1707) One of Bashō's most famous disciples; he is known for his sparkling wit and humour.

Uejima Onitsura (1661–1738) Famous for his philosophic approach and gentle humour. Onitsura once stated "outside truth, there is no poetry". Onitsura became a priest at the age of 73.

Konishi Raizan (1654–1716) A poet who lived in Osaka; he was famous during the Genroku period.

Masaoka Shiki (1867–1902) An extremely influential haiku poet and theorist, who successfully redefined the genre of haiku poetry during his brief life, gaining a loyal following.

Tan Taigi (1709–71) A prolific, accessible haiku poet who was a close associate of Buson.

FURTHER READING

Barnhill, D.L., trans. *Bashō's Journey: The Literary Prose of Matsuo Bashō*, State University of New York Press, Albany 2005

Collcutt, M., Jansen, M. and Kamakura, I. *Cultural Atlas of Japan*, Phaidon, Oxford 1988

Cobb, D., ed. *The British Museum Haiku*, The British Museum Press 2002

Eckel, M. D. *Understanding Buddhism*, Duncan Baird Publishers, London 2003 and Oxford University Press, New York 2002

Henderson, H.G. *Introduction to Haiku*, Doubleday Anchor Books, New York 1983

Levering, M. *Zen Inspirations*, Duncan Baird Publishers, London 2004

Littleton, C. S. *Understanding Shinto*, Duncan Baird Publishers, London 2002 and Oxford University Press, New York 2002

Lowenstein, T. *Buddhist Inspirations*, Duncan Baird Publishers, London 2005

Lowenstein, T. *Vision of the Buddha*, Duncan Baird Publishers, London 1996

Sato, H. and Watson, B. *From the Country of Eight Islands: An Anthology of Japanese Poetry*, University of Washington Press, Seattle 1981

Sosnoski, D., ed. *Introduction to Japanese Culture*, Charles E. Tuttle Company, Rutland, Vermont 1998

Stryk, L. and Ikemoto, T. *Penguin Book of Zen Poetry*, Penguin Books, London and New York 1981

Ueda, M. *Matsuo Bashō: The Master Haiku Poet,* Kondasha International, London and New York 1982

Yuasa, N., trans. *The Narrow Road to the Deep North and Other Travel Sketches*, Penguin, London and New York 2001

INDEX

Japanese names appear in
Japanese order: family name
preceding personal name.

PICTURE CREDITS

AA   The Art Archive, London
BAL The Bridgeman Art Library
BL   The British Library
BM   The Trustees of The British Museum

Page: 2 Photo.com; 14–15 Private Collection, Giraudon/ BAL;17 AA/Private Collection/Dagli Orti; 18 AA/Mitsui Collection Tokyo/Laurie Platt Winfrey; 22–23 Rubber Ball Productions/Getty Images; 27 AA/Kitano Temmangu Kyoto/Laurie Platt Winfrey; 30–31 Tony Sweet/Getty Images; 33 Museum of Fine Arts, Boston/BAL; 35 AA/Gunshots; 36–37 Rubber Ball Productions/Getty Images; 38–39 Museum of Fine Arts, Houston, Gift of Peter C. Knudtzon/BAL; 41 Leeds Museums and Art Galleries/BAL; 42–43 Tony Sweet/Getty Images; 44–45 BL; 47 Museum of Fine Arts, Houston, Gift of Peter C. Knudtzon/BAL; 48 Burstein Collection/Corbis; 50–51 Tony Sweet/Getty Images; 53 RMN/ Harry Bréjat ; 56 Asian Art & Archaeology, Inc./Corbis; 60–61 Tony Sweet /Getty Images; 63 Sakamoto Photo Research Laboratory/Corbis; 64 –65 Photo.com; 68–69 Rubber Ball Productions/Getty Images; 72–73 Eyewire Images; 74–75 Michael S. Yamashita/Corbis; 77 Chris Rainier/Corbis; 78 Getty Images; 80–81 Rubber Ball Productions/Getty Images; 82–83 BM; 86–87 Rubber Ball Productions/Getty Images; 89 Rubber Ball Productions/Getty Images; 92–93 Tony Sweet/Getty Images; 95 Michael Milton/Getty Images; 99 Chris Rainier/Corbis; 100–101 Tony Sweet/Getty Images; 102–3 Karen Kasmauski/Getty Images; 105 Brooklyn Museum of Art, New York, Gift of Anna Ferris/BAL; 108–109 Photo.com; 110 Michael Freeman/Corbis; 113 Royalty Free Corbis; 114–115 Tony Sweet/Getty Images; 116–117 Tony Sweet/Getty Images; 118 Tokyo Fuji Art Museum, Tokyo, Japan/BAL; 122–123 Tony Sweet /Getty Images; 124 RMN/Harry Brejat; 128–129 Tony Sweet/Getty Images; 130–131 Fitzwilliam Museum, University of Cambridge/BAL; 132 BL; 135 Ashmolean Museum, Oxford; 137 Christie's Images; 138–139 Photo.com; 140–141 Darrell Gulin/Corbis; 142 Emely/Zefa/Corbis; 147 AA/Private Collection/Dagli Orti; 149 Fitzwilliam Museum,University of Cambridge; 150–151 Tony Sweet/Getty Images

ACKNOWLEDGMENTS

Victoria James would like to thank the Daiwa Anglo-Japanese Foundation, especially Marie Conte-Helm, Junko Kono, Christopher Everett and Michael Thompson. The publishers would like to thank Hamish Todd and the Japanese Collections Department at the British Library for their invaluable support during this project, particularly in finding Japanese-language versions of the haiku.